this day, but would. Others from the New York press were present as well and they were appalled by what Jim had done to Ellen. Out of respect to Ellen, no one wrote about the incident, but Jim's reputation as Mr. Charm plummeted.

Patricia Kennealy and Fred Myrow viewed it more charitably. Patricia told me that when they shook hands, 'there were sparks, from the friction on the carpet'. She also admits to a different kind of spark that she felt in her heart, although it would be more than six months before they began their relationship. Fred Myrow, on the other hand, found in Jim a kindred soul with whom he identified immediately.

'When we met,' Fred said, 'he gave me the heaviest first line I've ever had: "Fred, if I don't find some way to develop within a year, all I'll be good for is nostalgia."' Fred had gone to the Philharmonic on a commission from the Dmitri Metropolis Foundation to write an evening of music that Leonard Bernstein would premier, based on an African primitive funeral ritual. While he had found this intellectually stimulating at the time, and now it was of interest to Jim Morrison, in time Fred came to question it. While doing a subsequent concert in Berlin, he heard the first Beatles album and began to think that what he was doing was 'out of joint with the outside world. There was a life and vitality in the Beatles' music which was not in my main line of work, which was giving concerts of avant-garde contemporary music. For two years I sat in the Carnegie Recital Hall and when I met Jim, I knew we both had to make a move. It cemented our relationship immediately.'

Back in Los Angeles, Jim turned his attention to the dramatic stage when the Living Theatre came to town for a week of performances at the University of Southern California. Jim had known of the revolutionary, communal theatrical troupe for some time, pumping the *Free Press* writer John Carpenter for details when he said he had a friend in the group; reading avidly an article about the actors and their founders, Julian Beck and Judith Malina, in *Ramparts* magazine; and finally from Michael McClure, who had known the Becks in New York ten years earlier. He asked the Doors' secretary to buy 16 front row tickets for each of the five performances.

Paradise Now was one of the troupe's most controversial performances and the one they decided to put on in Los Angeles. 'It's a play in which at the end of eight different sections, we play at each section an encounter with the audience,' Judith told me. 'We bring up a category of subjects. We're all on the stage together, rapping, having all kinds of encounters and relationships. Sometimes I'll be with two people in a relationship in one scene and Julian will be somewhere else in the theatre in another scene. The tone is very aggressive. Sometimes that aggression is very positive. Sometimes it isn't. But our intention is to turn it into something very positive, take it to paradise by bringing out all the hostilities.'

Julian added, 'The play also traces different revolutionary steps. The effort is to go from one step . . . one run, to another . . . and keep carrying the public along. We challenge the public to play different roles.'

The roles came out of rules, they said – like not being able to travel from one country to another without a passport, and not being able to live without money, and not being able to smoke marijuana, and not being able to embrace nudity. As indicated by the Becks, the play changed substantially from performance to performance, but the structure remained, along with some of the more powerful scenes. Each night at the end of the performance, different cast members cried out:

'I'm not allowed to take my clothes off!'

'The body itself of which we are made is taboo!'

'We are ashamed of what is most beautiful, we are afraid of what is most beautiful!'

'We may not act naturally toward one another!'

'The culture represses love!'

'I am not allowed to take my clothes off!'

It was at this point that the actors stripped down to their underwear, making the point that they had reached society's limit. They then cried, 'I'm not allowed to take my clothes off! I am outside the Gates of Paradise!'

That was when the Los Angeles Police Department moved in and stopped the performance. Jim was sitting in the front row. The next day the Doors were scheduled to appear in Miami.

V

The Drunk

Jim was drunk when he arrived at Miami's Dinner Key Auditorium.

He was late and the Doors and the audience, which was crushed into a large open space without chairs, were restless. The Doors had agreed to accept $25,000 for the show, instead of the usual 60% of the gross, when they were assured that the gross wouldn't exceed $42,000. Then the seats were taken out by the producers, allowing them to sell an extra 7,000 tickets, and when the Doors discovered the awful conditions in the auditorium, they were outraged. So when Jim finally arrived, the tension between the producers and the Doors was substantial while the conditions on the auditorium floor were worsening. All those bodies packed into a space too small began to generate a collective heat that blended with the assorted drugs thousands in the audience had ingested or smoked before entering.

The tape I have of the concert reveals two things: (1) Jim was entirely too drunk to perform, and (2) the 'performance' he gave more or less followed the outline of the Living Theatre's play, *Paradise Now*, almost as if it were scripted. Over the next hour, the Doors repeatedly tried to get Jim on track musically, starting and abandoning several songs when Jim was unwilling, or unable, to sing. While Jim interacted with the audience, sharing drinks with the ones closest to the stage, then standing up and bellowing, 'I'm not talking about a revolution! I'm talking about having a good time!'

Within ten minutes Jim turned the plea for a good time into an awful time. It started when he told the audience, 'I'm lonely. I need some love, you all. Come on. I need some good times. I want some love-ah, love-ah. Ain't nobody gonna come up here and love me, huh? Ain't nobody gonna love my ass? Come on!'

And that quickly degenerated into Jim calling the audience 'a bunch of fuckin' idiots'. What happened after that is debatable. In *No One Here Gets Out Alive*, I took the position that Jim did not expose himself, as he was later charged by Miami police. Vince Treanor, the band's road manager, was on the stage behind Jim and he said that when Jim unzipped his leather pants, he was wearing bulky boxer shorts underneath them – unusual for Jim, because he rarely wore underwear. Vince said it was Jim's intention to go only so far, just as the Living Theatre had done, then stop. Besides that, Vince said, he crouched behind Jim put a hand against Jim's back and pulled back on his belt, making it impossible for Jim to lower his pants.

There were others who testified differently. They said Jim definitely exposed himself. Not long ago, I heard from a young woman who said she was present at the concert and in a four-page letter she insisted that it was true; she remembered Jim's penis, after all these years, vividly.

The weird thing is that none of the charges against Jim were filed for several days. In fact, during the performance, Jim had removed a police officer's hat and sailed it into the audience like a Frisbee. Backstage, the officer laughed and appeared to enjoy meeting the band, as Billy Siddons gave him a couple of hundred dollars for the hat.

Jim was vacationing in the Caribbean when, on March 5th, 1969, the Dade County Sheriff's office issued a warrant for his arrest, charging him with lewd and lascivious behaviour (a felony), indecent exposure, open profanity, and drunkenness (all misdemeanours). A day later he added another charge, simulated oral copulation on his guitar player, Robby Krieger. At some point during the evening, when Robby was performing a solo, Jim had dropped to his knees in front of him, someone had taken a picture, and that was regarded as evidence that Jim was mimicking a sexual act.

At first the Doors thought it was a joke and even when they realized it wasn't, it was a while before they took it seriously. After all, this wasn't the first time. No one had forgotten New

Haven. As Ray recalled, 'There wasn't anything he did in Miami he hadn't done a lot of other times.'

Besides, drama was a part of this game, an integral part of every Doors act, on and off the stage. The destroyed recording studio in 1967 and the damaged hotel rooms since. The scenes with the swarming groupies. The soaring roar of love that greeted the Doors in concert. The hundreds of thousands of dollars that came washing in. Jim's mythic drunks. It was all so larger than life. What the hell difference did another drunken performance in another city mean?

As it turned out, it meant virtually everything. By the end of March, the FBI entered the case, charging Jim with unlawful flight from the country (to the Caribbean for his vacation following the Miami concert). It was a made-up charge, like the one saying he was trying to have oral sex with Robby.

At the same time, a 'decency' movement blossomed in Miami, evolving into a show at the Orange Bowl starring Anita Bryant and Jackie Gleason, assailing the Doors and everything their lead singer allegedly personified. The movement received national attention and the media started running long stories about the foul-mouthed, pants-dropping Jim Morrison. Not only the media, but the trade press as well, including *Boxoffice*, a monthly newsletter that went out to all the concert hall managers in the country. According to Billy Siddons, in the next month the Doors lost a million dollars in bookings.

'The word was out,' Ray Manzarek told me. 'Get the Doors.'

For Jim, it was a blessing in disguise. While he hated the injustice as much as the others, the cancelled concerts gave him precious time to work on his other projects and in the months that followed, he privately published two collections of his early poetry. He called his books *The Lords* and *The New Creatures*.

The first was no more than tastefully reproduced and packaged pages from his leftover UCLA notebooks, recording his eyeball-slashing thoughts about film. It was produced on 82 sheets of expensive paper stock and unbound, contained in a royal blue box that you folded around the poems and tied with a ribbon. The second book measured only four inches by

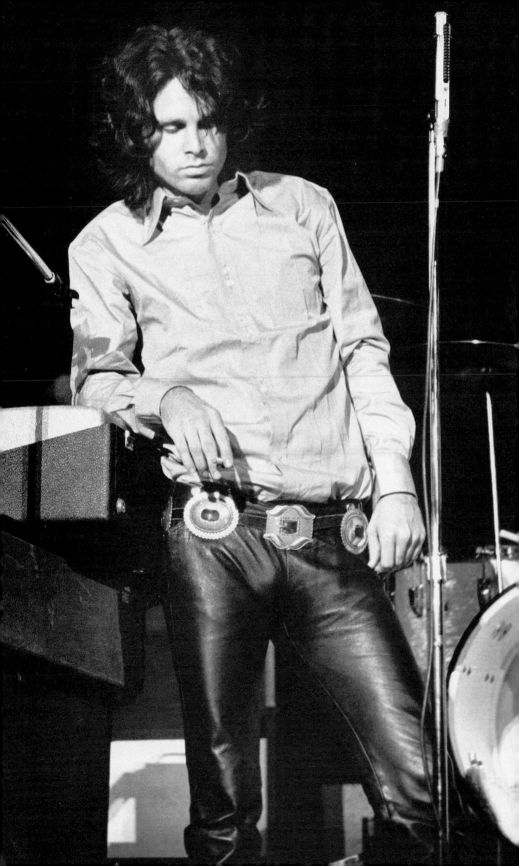

five and was bound in a simple brown cover reminiscent of school workbooks. The titles were embossed in gold and the author was identified as 'James Douglas Morrison'. He had 100 copies of each printed and for a long time, most of them were stacked against a wall in the Doors office. Nonetheless, Jim was thrilled.

During the same period, Jim also changed his image and agreed to do two key interviews. One was with me, for *Rolling Stone*. After Miami, *Rolling Stone* had depicted Jim as a buffoon and I knew he was more, or less, than that. At that time, *Rolling Stone* ran something called 'The Rolling Stone Interview' – inspired by the *Playboy* interviews, which appeared in question-and-answer form. Jim had never been interviewed by *Rolling Stone* in that fashion. I suggested to the editor, Jann Wenner, that we 'do' Jim. He agreed and after some consideration, Jim also agreed, and we got together over a tape recorder off and on for two weeks, over lunch, and over lots of beer.

The interview appears elsewhere in this book, so I won't go into it now, except to say that Jim remained intelligent and articulate from start to finish and he never got out of line. He got drunk, but never outrageous, or violent. I don't know if this was intentional, or lucky. I suspect it was intentional. Now that he had *Rolling Stone*'s attention, he was determined to charm, to rectify, and clarify.

After one of the interview sessions, conducted in the Doors' office, Jim suggested we go next door to the Phone Booth for a drink. As soon as we entered the club, 'Love Me Two Times' dropped onto the turntable and one of the topless dancers began to shake her two times for Jim. After the dance, Jim called her over and shyly introduced me as his friend. I confess being much more impressed by the dancer's thoracic development than by Jim's hyperbolic friendliness.

The last interview session ended in a recording studio, where Jim read the text of his latest poem, 'American Prayer' (which also would be privately published some months later). He asked that the poem run in *Rolling Stone* next to the inter-

A moment of contemplation: Minneapolis, 1968.

view and suggested that perhaps the Doors would be interested in promoting their next album by letting me interview them and releasing excerpts as radio spots. I admit I was flattered, although I didn't think it was a serious suggestion. Which it wasn't. And the poem was published with the interview, copyright by James Douglas Morrison.

Jim wanted to be taken seriously. Getting some of his ideas across, and appearing to be rational and intelligent in *Rolling Stone* represented a large step in that direction. *Rolling Stone* wasn't even two years old, but it was regarded as the hippest publication of the sixties, an arbiter of the culture, and its approval could be equated to the *Good Housekeeping* seal.

I came away from the interview liking Jim. He was playful. He had a sense of humour about himself. We were talking one day and he smiled and said, 'This is really a strange way to make a living isn't it?' I believe he meant it.

The other important interview he gave was for Channel 13, WNET in New York. Nowadays we call this kind of television PBS. Then we called it 'Educational Television'. And that's why Jim was there, to meet the hip New York press and to 'educate' them and the hip New York audience.

The show, *Critique*, opened with the Doors performing their newest single release, 'Tell All the People', a song of Robby Krieger's that Jim disagreed with so much that for the first time he insisted that individual writing credits appear on the recording. (Royalties remained evenly shared, as always.) He said it made him sound like he wanted people to follow him. Jim had decided early in life not to trust leaders and a leader is the last thing he wanted to be.

There followed a collection of songs that spanned most of the Doors' career, and this, in turn, was succeeded by a pyrotechnical, adjective-to-the-floor statement by Richard Goldstein, who had been one of the Doors' most avid champions in the *Village Voice* and other publications in the early days. He said the Doors had become so popular, they were 'able to leap tall groupies in a single bound' and then quoted Jim, saying, 'When you make your peace with authority, you become an authority.' Richie then introduced excerpts from an interview he did with the Doors a week earlier. In this, he referred to a story he wrote called 'The Shaman as Superstar'. He asked Jim if he thought rock heroes could perform a 'religious function for kids, for young people'.

Jim said he had read about the shaman and thought the shaman emerged because the people of his tribe pushed him into it. Richie said he thought a shaman was needed in a time of social turmoil, an obvious reference to the huge political and social battle being waged over Vietnam, sex, drugs, rock and roll, and a hundred other things at the time.

Jim said, 'I don't think the shaman, from what I've read, is really too interested in defining his role in society, he's just more interested in pursuing his own fantasies.'

The words came like beads on a string: well-formed, and orderly. It appeared clear that Jim was thinking. Surely, not everyone was able to follow him, but he was interesting.

His visual image was worth noting, too. Gone were the leather pants, replaced by baggy striped jeans. Always lean, now he had a obvious paunch, the dubious trophy that booze awards. That strong jaw and those beautiful sunken cheeks now resided behind a full beard. With his thin cigar and sunglasses, Jim now looked like a hip, fat Che Guevara. Gone was the rock hero that Richie wanted to talk about.

The show closed with Jim's performance of 'The Soft Parade', a long song-poem that was named for Jim's description of people walking along Sunset Boulevard, giving the Doors' new album its title. This album, recorded the previous winter, and released in July 1969, was not one of the group's best. The Doors themselves came to regard the album as the one they did with 'the La Cienega Symphony', named for the avenue that passed the Elektra studios and for the many classical musicians hired to provide backup on several of the songs, most notably on 'Touch Me', another Robby Krieger song that went to Number 1. (Ironically, Robby had called the song 'Hit Me', a bitter response to a faltering relationship with a woman, and it was Jim who suggested changing 'hit' to 'touch'.)

The Doors were not the only band to incorporate classical back-up during this period. But they probably were the least suited to it. The distinctive Doors sound was noted for its compelling coarseness and for its theatrical silences. With strings added, there were no silences and the gritty blues were diluted, and the Doors crossed over from rock to pop. In a word, they were overproduced. However, the album sold well. The Doors were an established commercial success, Miami or no Miami – perhaps, in part, because of Miami.

Actually, Miami was becoming a very big deal. When the Doors finally started to get work again, there was something new in the contracts. A special rider specified that if Jim was obscene, or profane, the Doors would be liable for damages. And, the Doors were informed, police would be waiting in the wings with arrest warrants all filled in – all they had to do was write in the charges and arrest Jim on the spot.

'A "fuck clause",' Jim said when he was told about it. 'I bet it's a rock and roll first.'

One of the first big concerts was set for Mexico in June. The Doors were to play the Plaza Monumental, which was Mexico City's biggest bull ring, as its name implied. The idea was to charge only 40 cents to a dollar admission, so the kids of the city could attend. I was the only writer invited to go along (for *Rolling Stone*). I remember visiting the Doors' office the night before scheduled departure. Mario Olmos, the concert promoter, arrived at the office with a $20,000 cashier's cheque and told Billy Siddons and the others that the performance wasn't going to be in the bull ring, it was going to be in a large night club comparable to the Copa in New York or the Ambassador Hotel in Los Angeles. Olmos, who brought Javier Castro, the owner of the Forum, with him, said he just hadn't been able to get all the permits necessary. As in America, there had been student riots in Mexico City and the government didn't want that many young people collected in one place at the same time. The Doors had not been consulted about this venue change and they didn't like it.

The small office was lighted by candles, empty beer bottles were scattered around, and everybody was saying things like, 'Fuck it, we won't go.' Mario explained that it wasn't his fault,

On stage, Jim could manipulate the audience with silence.

and it probably wasn't, at least not entirely, and eventually Jim and the others changed their minds and went home to finish packing. The next day we were on a plane with thousands of pounds of sound equipment.

We stayed in a nice motel built around a swimming pool in a nice section of the city, not far from the archaeological museum. (Very classy by Mexico City standards, the guard at the gate had a silver-handled pistol in his holster and a little custom-made waterproof cover for the handle when it rained.) We were given a translator, a bright woman with even more class than the motel had, and a pair of black and white Cadillac limousines were made available 24 hours a day.

After we arrived, Jim asked if I would switch rooms with him, which I did. Later that night, of course, Pam called and the switchboard put her through to me. Which was Jim's plan all along. So I told her she had the wrong room and I gave her the right one and got the switchboard back. Next morning, Jim smiled at me and said, 'You really know how to hurt a guy.'

Jim remained playful throughout the week. The first night he and I shared the white limo, while the other three Doors travelled in the black one. As we approached the club, I saw a fifteen-foot-high painting of Jim's face on the wall of the front of the club. It didn't look like the bearded Jim at all.

The other Doors alighted from the black Cadillac and were greeted by screams from the fans clustered near the stage entrance. No one paid any attention as Jim left our car. He wasn't recognized. He chuckled and called out to the fans, 'Hey! Over here! Give the singer some.'

Before the show, I sat with Billy Siddons at a nearby cafe. Billy told me he was very unhappy about Jim's refusal to shave his beard. He said he had asked Jim to shave, but he refused.

The performances were good and well received. 'The End', as it turned out, was the Doors' biggest hit in Mexico, for reasons that experts in Catholicism and macho lifestyles will have to sort out. When Jim got to the line, 'Father I want to kill you/Mother I want to...,' all the young men in the audience finished the lyric for him, at the top of their voices. We also discovered that the song was a staple in Mexico City juke boxes and usually had been played so frequently, it was worn right down to the white plastic interior.

For the full week, Jim was on his best behaviour. Mainly he stayed by himself, reading. When he did go out, he was approachable, friendly, using his high school Spanish to communicate with the local fans. The day we went to the archaeological museum, he paired off with a young redhead, an American woman who was known to be one of the 'Presidential groupies', the band of mainly American women who had attached themselves to the President's son. Another day, we went to a park where the mariachis performed and Jim and I got drunk together and he paid an extravagant sum for a waiter's wooden serving tray. Still another night, as we were returning to the motel from the club, again he was a little drunk and as the chauffeur pushed the speedometer to 80, slowing to 50 for the right angle turns, Jim leaned out of the limo and pointed his finger like a pistol.

'Andele! (Hurry!),' he shouted into the night. 'Bang . . . bang . . . bang! Andele! Andele!' A bandit riding with Zapata's ghost in a Cadillac along the Avenue de la Revolucion on a sultry Mexican night.

In the year that followed, only a few of the times I saw Jim had anything to do with rock and roll. Now he invited me to poetry readings, and screenings of films he thought I'd enjoy. One of the readings – at which Jim read some of his poems – with Michael McClure – was a fund-raiser for Norman Mailer, who was running for mayor of New York.

Other times we met at Barney's Beanery and drank, talking about writing and writers. I was by now working on an Elvis Presley book for Simon & Schuster – the book that Jim suggested – and we shared the same editor, so we had a common meeting ground. There was a picture taken of Jim during the Miami concert, in his leather hat with the skull and crossbones on the hat band; Jim's eyes were closed and he was bearded. Jim told me that he had told his editor he wanted that photograph on the cover of the book. The editor argued gently for a picture that would be more recognizable. Jim was watching his own poetry move through the editing process.

*Long before the Miami scandal, Jim's performance
style was designed to shock and titillate.*

The Drunk

'He was so serious,' the editor, Jonathan Dolger, told me. 'He'd had so many rejections on his poetry. He wasn't concerned at all with money. We didn't pay him much. He was concerned with the look of the book and with the tastefulness of the way the book was published. It was important that I take him seriously as a writer.

'I found his poetry interesting. Some of it's very bad. I suggested taking some of it out, but he didn't. We changed the order. I made some suggestions. *The Lords* was not so good and I thought we should cut some of that out. He didn't want that particularly, but we did some reorganizing.'

In the late summer and fall of 1989, Jim rented first the second and then the ground floor of a building across the street from the Elektra offices. Babe and Frank and Paul and anyone who had anything to do with the documentary film – still being edited – occupied the second floor space. The ground floor was for Pamela and a boutique she was planning, which eventually cost Jim more than $250,000.

They still fought as passionately as they loved and both continued to spend a lot of time with other sexual partners. One of Jim's long-time drinking friends, Tom Baker, was still around and he remembered that when they went to the rock clubs on the Sunset Strip, 'Morrison was usually in a stupor and seemed oblivious to the fans. As soon as we sat down, the resident groupies would pounce on him. Sometimes I would share in the spoils. Other times I would be ignored as though I were invisible. Still other times Jim would be so comatose I would get them all to myself.

'One night we went to the grim little Hollywood flat of two of these creatures and sat up till dawn drinking and talking. One girl soon revealed herself to be a practising junkie and she brought out a plastic vial of pills, blue tablets called New Morthone, a strong synthetic morphine. We crushed them with a tablespoon and sniffed the powder. The high was speedy and euphoric and Jim became loose and talkative, telling us endless tales about himself, including the story of his body being inhabited by the spirit of an old Indian dying by the side of a New Mexico highway.

'After a while, I went to bed in the front room with the

junkie and the other girl began to wrestle Jim into her bedroom. He had become somewhat inert and sat with his head
on the kitchen table. After a great effort, she got him into her
bed and shut the door. About ten minutes later, she joined the
junkie and me, complaining about Jim's lack of interest. Soon,
the three of us were engaged in a robust bout of interchanging
sexual positions and then I passed out, exhausted and content.

'I awoke at the crack of noon, alone. I sat in the kitchen
drinking instant coffee and smoking cigarettes for about fifteen minutes. Then curiosity got the best of me and I slowly
opened the bedroom door and looked in. The little beggars
had abandoned me for Jim, and he and the junkie were asleep
alongside one another. The other girl was feverishly giving
Jim head, trying to pump some life into his pathetically limp
dick. She looked not unlike a young lioness feeding on her
fallen prey. She glanced over at me for a moment, then went
right back to work. I returned to the kitchen and crushed up
another pill.'

Pam and Jim took a second-floor apartment in a two-storey
building on Norton Avenue, not far from Barney's Beanery.
Diane Gardiner, who had stopped doing publicity for the
Doors, lived in an apartment downstairs. 'They were amusing
neighbours,' Diane told me. 'Also dramatic. They lived a
swashbuckling kind of existence. Their stairway came down
to my doorway and they'd have fights up and down the stairs,
like Errol Flynn. Then Jim would throw his books out the window. The next morning he would pick up his books and move
back in again.

'One time Pamela took me to Rive Gauche in Beverly Hills,
where she bought $5,000 worth of clothes. She'd run off to the
dressing room, hissing at me, "He owes me this! He owes me
this!" '

It was never boring. Always, drama was in the room, or in
an adjacent one. Jay Sebring, the hair stylist who had shaped
Jim's leonine look back in 1967, was one of the people killed
with Sharon Tate by Charlie Manson's gang. That was in the
late summer of 1969. And that was when the Woodstock generation took one step forward and two steps back. The
Woodstock gathering was in August, becoming an instant

myth for the decade, and when only a couple of months later, the Rolling Stones hired the Hell's Angels to provide security at a free concert in Altamont, California, and they beat a naked, fat boy to death with pool cues, they symbolically killed everyone.

Elektra was demanding more product, wanted a new album by Christmas. To everyone's amazement, the band produced one of the best of the Doors' career. *Morrison Hotel*, named for a $2.50-a-night hotel in skid row Los Angeles (in front of which the group posed for a photograph), contained a substantial body of fair poetry and some of the band's best blues.

Some of the strongest stuff came from something Ray found in one of Jim's notebooks titled 'Abortion Stories'. This included references to blood running in the streets of Chicago, 'blood in my love in the terrible summer, bloody red sun of Phantastic L.A.'. The title given the song, 'Peace Frog', was ludicrous, but the message was strong. This song also contained Jim's only recorded reference to the much-told story from his childhood, when he witnessed Indians dying along a New Mexico highway.

By now, Jim had bought a cottage for Pam in Topanga Canyon behind a country bar and club, so he wrote a song called 'Roadhouse Blues'. It was one of several songs inspired at least in part by Pamela and the one song that best captured Jim's live-fast-die-young-and-make-a-good-looking-corpse philosophy.

The 'La Cienega symphony' was history and the apocalyptic Doors were back. The singles selected for release from the album, 'Running Blue' and 'You Make Me Real', sold poorly, but *Morrison Hotel* was another major hit, becoming the fifth album in a row to sell more than a million copies. This was a first for an American band.

In November, 1969, Jim flew to Phoenix with Tom Baker to see the Rolling Stones in concert. They were drunk, of course, and en route they started throwing things around the cabin and harassing the flight crew. This led to their being arrested by the FBI upon landing and charged with being drunk and disorderly and interfering with the flight of an aircraft, an offence under the 'skyjacking' law that could lead to a $10,000 fine and a ten-year sentence.

The same month, Jim appeared in Miami in Judge Murray Goodman's courtroom to plead not guilty to the charges that came out of the concert in March. Trial was set for April 1970. In the following months, as Jim and his lawyers spent more and more time planning his defence, and Billy Siddons tried to get the Doors back into the concert halls, Jim tried to get something going in film. His words to Fred Myrow seemed to be echoing in his mind every day: 'If I don't find a new way to develop creatively within a year, I'll be good for nothing but nostalgia.' However much others insisted he continue with his music career, however often he was drunk – and by now it was almost an everyday occurrence – his goal stayed fixed in place, clear, commanding, immutable.

Jim and his friends had completed a short 'feature' called *HWY*. If it left the viewer desiring resolution, it also was a compelling work. On the one hand it was little more than a student's film, impressionistic and deliberately quirky, but it had been filmed slowly and on a comfortable budget, which gave it a sense of professionalism, and with Jim's peculiar mind serving as the engine, it produced a mysterious, almost mystical look into a killer's mind. Jim was virtually the only actor in the film and its director.

He was a hitchhiker in the desert. He got a ride and then, suddenly, the driver of the car was gone and Jim was behind the wheel. What happened to the driver was not explained, only hinted at. In one scene, Jim entered a telephone booth and told someone, 'I wasted him.' (As a practical joke, Jim actually called Michael McClure in the scene, and never explained; all McClure ever heard was Jim saying, 'I wasted him,' then hang up. He figured Jim was drunk and forgot about it.) In the film, Jim then drove into L.A. and there was a lot of footage of bars and cars and cops at night. The movie ended ambiguously.

Over the months that followed, everyone who saw it commented favourably on Jim's presence, or charisma, but thought the film little more than an academic joke; it was, like Jim's film at UCLA, short, without plot, and strange.

On stage in Miami: Jim and Robby Krieger.

Therefore, without commercial potential.

During the same period, Jim met with Timothy Leary to talk about documenting his run for the California governorship, but Leary was thrown into jail, aborting the project. Efforts to make a deal with Carlos Casteneda to film his book, *The Teachings of Don Juan*, were no more successful, and when Steve McQueen considered Jim for a role in a film called *Adam at 6 P.M.*, Jim was rejected because the producers thought his drinking would be a liability.

There were a couple of good concerts in January 1970, followed by meetings with Elektra in New York. A young publicist with Rogers & Cowan, the publicity firm that had represented them from the start, had come up with a new campaign, in which Jim would be promoted as a 'renaissance man'. Poet. Lyricist. Singer. Actor. Director. The memorandum from the company files showed that its author believed it was necessary for Jim to be comfortable with the concept, but it ended with a note that turned Jim off completely: 'There aren't any Leonardos on the scene, and they'll love it in Poughkeepsie.'

The Doors were in New York to perform at the Felt Forum, a concert hall connected to Madison Square Garden. There was a party following the last of four shows, hosted by Elektra Records. The Doors' contract was about to expire and it was typical for record companies in such a situation to show sudden and expensive interest. It was the perfect party, with all the right people, the best food, and a screening of Alfred Hitchcock's *The Thirty-Nine Steps*. On the way out, Pamela, on Jim's arm, told Jac Holzman, 'Well, in case we're on Atlantic next year, thanks for the swell party.' The 'renaissance man' idea was dropped and the Doors renewed their Elektra contract, promising one more album.

The funny thing is, the 'renaissance man' concept wasn't inappropriate, only badly motivated from Jim's point of view – and perhaps a little pretentious. Surely Jim was wise to decline. Living down the Lizard King label was hard enough; he wasn't about to wear DaVinci's cloak.

By late February 1970, Jim had started meeting with Jim Aubry, the one-time programming chief at CBS TV, now between jobs but soon to be president of MGM. After their first meeting, Aubry turned to an assistant and said, 'Jim Morrison's going to be the biggest motion picture star of the next ten years. He's going to be the James Dean of the seventies.' He told his assistant to sign Jim to a contract at any cost and that resulted in an agreement to have Jim work with Michael McClure in turning Michael's unpublished novel, *The Adept*, into a screenplay.

Aubry's assistant was Bill Bellasco, a former agent whose company, St. Regis Films, was the joint venture partner in the project with Jim's company, HiWay Productions. 'Aubry's interest in Jim was in his overall creative abilities,' Belasco told me. 'Jim was co-writing the script with McClure and Jim and I were going to co-produce the film and Jim was going to be the star. Aubry and I had a hunch about Jim that if he could ever be harnessed, he could be a film maker. Whether that meant director, writer, or producer, or a combination, we didn't know. The problem of course was discipline.'

According to Michael McClure, discipline *wasn't* a problem, at least not for as long as he was involved. An office was provided in the 9000 Sunset Building and McClure said they kept regular hours. 'Jim was hung-over and late a few times, I was the same,' he said. 'But generally we started at 9:30, worked until 12:30, took off for an hour, came back and worked until 4:30 or 5:30. This went on for six weeks. We turned out a script that was longer than the novel. It looked like somebody shot the manuscript of *Moby Dick* out of a cannon.'

As the script was being written, Aubry moved into the president's office at MGM and Jim began meeting with directors, including Sam Fuller, a seasoned veteran known mainly for his action B-movies but regarded by some as one of the most influential film makers of the post-war period. He was a hard drinker, too, and while Jim had great respect for his talent, ultimately Fuller was found to be unacceptable by MGM.

Taking his place was Ted Flicker, the young director of the Premise Players, a group of maverick satirists who came to Hollywood in the early 1960s. By 1967, Flicker had written and directed the vastly under-appreciated satire, *The President's Analyst*.

At the same time, Aubry was trying to get Jim to take an acting role in another film while the script was being completed. Jim read several scripts, but turned them down. Today, McClure thinks the screenwriting assignment was merely 'a way for Jim to get into the movies. We all got what we wanted. Belasco was doing his producer bit, Aubry thought he was getting Jim as an actor, and we were learning how to write a film script and thought we were into a real project.'

As Belasco remembered it, the film began to fall apart by mid-summer. The script, now called *St Nicholas*, named for the major character, a dope dealer, had been cut from 'something two inches thick to 90 flimsy pages. I was there when it was cut. The winnowing down was done in two days. Winnowing down? It was an amputation.'

The Doors were another hospital case. While Billy Siddons was now able to find them more bookings, everyone I talked to agreed that the relationship between Jim and the others was strained.

Belasco said, 'The conflict grew out of the Miami incident, for which they all held Jim responsible and they'd begun to do numbers in their own heads that he had ruined their careers. Which I always resented, because they wouldn't have had careers if it hadn't been for Jim Morrison. So he was carrying the whole burden on his back. And they were making it uncomfortable for him. However irresponsible Jim may have been, they had a responsibility to him, because he made the group. They knew going in he was not responsible by their standards. When the money was rolling in, nobody complained. When things went wrong, caused by that same frenetic personality that made things right earlier, everybody ran away.'

Aubry among others tried to convince Jim to leave the band. It was no secret that Atlantic Records wanted him. MGM Records also wanted Jim, alone, and Belasco tried to

Moments after the infamous Miami concert ends,
Morrison emerges from his dressing room to stare
down trance-like at the chaos below.

talk him into making the move. 'He could've made millions alone,' Bellasco said. But Jim refused to act. Though he may not have had anything other than his livelihood in common with the other three members of the group, he remained loyal.

One reason may have been that he needed the money. Much of 1970 was devoted not to film, or music, but to jurisprudence and his lawyer, Max Fink, was not cheap; people in the Doors camp told me that the Miami trial probably cost Jim a half a million dollars.

The Phoenix trial in March was another cost. Jim was clean-shaven now and, like Tom Baker, dressed neatly in a white shirt. One of the stewardesses said she had been mauled by one of the defendants, but 'the girls had Jim and me confused,' Baker said. 'Everyone else who testified, including the other government witnessses, contradicted them, but the judge accepted their word along with the claim that Jim made an obscene gesture toward Sherry Ann and uttered the "pussy" word. So, based on the cockamamie testimony of these two airheads, Jim was convicted of a misdemeanour, and I was totally acquitted. Jim was confused, because if anyone made a move, it was done by whoever was sitting in my seat.'

That night, Jim and Baker got drunk with the Phoenix lawyer who had joined Max Fink in the defence. They 'started talking about calling Sherry Ann and her friend. The lawyer could not believe we would have anything to do with them after they tried to put us in jail. I told him we were really going to get back at them by taking them out into the desert and fucking them and leaving them there. Jim and I exchanged broad winks, then he said not only would we strip them and fuck them, but we would urinate on their bare bodies before deserting them. The lawyer was cockeyed drunk and crawling around on his hands and knees, pleading with us not to do it. He looked pathetic and we laughed at him and tormented him until he passed out.'

The party continued in Los Angeles when they returned, concluding the following night with Jim and Tom punching it out in the Doors' office. Jim ended up calling the sheriff's office on Tom and when they came, seeing who was involved, they told the boys to go home and sleep it off. Later that night,

Tom heaved a rock through the Doors' office window. Jim did not speak for Tom for the next eight months.

The Miami trial was traumatic in a much different way. Max Fink prepared a 63-page document worthy of publication in a legal journal, connecting dozens of legal cases involving films such as *I Am Curious, Yellow* and *Midnight Cowboy*, the art of Gauguin and Michelangelo, and the First, Eighth and Fourteenth Amendments to the Constitution. Of the four laws that Jim was charged with breaking, the most recent had been enacted in 1918, and Max and Jim fully expected to be able to introduce the concept of 'contemporary community standards'. Max wanted jurors to be able to see *Hair* and some of the comedians performing in Miami's clubs.

They were wrong. In August, when the trial began, Judge Hoffman was getting ready for a tough re-election campaign in the fall and it appeared that Jim's trial was a part of his campaign. All of Max's petitions were denied and the 63-page brief was disregarded.

Harvey Perr was a young playwright who worked from time to time for Elektra as a publicist. After listening to the tapes of the Miami concert, he believed that Jim's performance had been a statement.

'It was very rhythmic,' he told me. 'I mean, for all the obscenity, he was really telling the audience to revolt, to revolt against the overpriced tickets, to revolt against the system, and to love each other. He said: "Fuck your neighbour, fuck your neighbour." It all had a rhythm, almost like one of his poems. It was like this big, brawling, drunken poem, telling them to revolt. And it really seemed to me to come out of that spirit that he had got at the Living Theatre. I mentioned that to him and he thought that was very perceptive. It was I think very important for him that he was doing something very consciously from the beginning that he felt was revolutionary. Once the judge denied all of Max's motions, Jim wasn't interested any more.'

Mike Gershman, the Doors' first publicist, who hadn't represented the group in some time, was employed to handle the trial press. The thing that surprised him was that the national press was about as interested in covering the trial

	I.	**LEWD AND LASCIVIOUS BEHAVIOR (FEL)**
	II.	**INDECENT EXPOSURE (MISD)**
	III.	**OPEN PROFANITY (MISD)**
TO: THE DADE COUNTY SHERIFF'S OFFICE	CHARGE IV.	**DRUNKENNESS (MISD)**

Defendant **TO BE ARRESTED**

JAMES MORRISON

Name of Defendant

69— 2355

Race **W** Sex **M** Age _____

Address _____ Phone _____

Height _____ Weight _____

Business Address _____ Phone _____
**Member of musical group
(The Doors)**

Occupation or Business

Hair _____ Eyes _____

Complexion _____

3/1/69 **Dinner Key Auditorium**

Date of Offense _____ Location of Offense

Marks or
Features _____

REMARKS: **Booking Agent for "The Doors" is**

Comments _____

Ashley Famous Agency, 1301 Ave. of the

FILED

MAR 5 1969

J. F. McCRACKEN

Americas, New York City, New York

CLERK

Complainant (s) (Note: If filed by an officer, both the name of the victim and of the department are shown below)

Bob Jennings, 495 NW 93rd St.

Name **Theodore Seaman, MPD** Address _____ Phone _____

ASSISTANT STATE ATTORNEY: **ALFONSO C. SEPE** alc

201.01—5

*A copy of the warrant for Jim's arrest issued by
Dade County Sheriff's office, 1969. He was
accused of lewd and lascivious behaviour, indecent
exposure, open profanity and drunkenness.*

as the judge was interested in hearing Max's arguments.

'So here we go to Miami to what could and should have been a very pivotal political trial and at the time as a publicist, I remember banging my head against the wall, writing to all the *Times* and *Newsweeks* and so on about coverage, and *Rolling Stone* and all the rock papers and everybody. And nobody was interested. I wrote a series of articles for *Rock* magazine. One was called 'Apathy for the Devil' [a play on the title of the Rolling Stones' recent album, *Sympathy for the Devil*] which put it into perspective. Woodstock had happened the previous year. To me, the exposure was a tremendously political issue and I couldn't get through to people, to make them understand it. I was in Miami for three weeks for the trial.

The Drunk

Morrison stands outside the Miami courtroom
after being sentenced to 6 months in jail and fined
$500 for indecent exposure and public profanity,
October 1970.

Gloria Vanjeck did a piece for *Stone*. I did the series for *Rock*.
But that was it.'

There was another disappointment for Jim. Not even his
local fans supported him. 'The trial was "the afternoon of a
superstar,"' Gershman said. 'The first day, a hundred kids
showed up at nine in the morning. Second day it was forty.
Third day it was twelve.'

It also appeared that Jim was being railroaded. If Phoenix
had been odd, Miami was no less than bizarre. One day, the
prosecutor brought a Doors album into the courtroom and
asked Jim to autograph it. Another day, he handed Jim a piece
of paper on which he had written a limerick:

139

'There once was a group called the Doors
Who sang in dissent of the mores
To youth they protested
As witnesses attested
While the leader was dropping his drawers.'

The prosecution's witnesses were ludicrous. They presented a picture of chaste and offended middle-America, a perfect
follow-up to the Orange Bowl rally against indecency that had
followed the concert, a comforting, flag-waving vehicle for the
judge's re-election campaign. Teenagers in pony-tails testified
as to how shocked they were by Jim's performance and moth-
ers of those teenagers spluttered their indignation. There
were seventeen witnesses in all and virtually every one of
them either worked in or was related to someone who worked
in the prosecutor's office or for the police department.

Midway through the trial, the prosecution offered a deal.
Said Gershman, 'If Jim would do a free concert, not at the
Orange Bowl, because they had the decency rally, if he gave a
concert, at Brandon Park, I think, and gave the proceeds to
their anti-drug thing in Miami, the City's drug abuse programme, they'd drop everything except one misdemeanour,
which would mean a suspended sentence. I guess it was
drunkenness or abusive language. The deal was considered
for a couple of days and turned down.'

Jim sat calmly through it all, drawing pictures of the witnesses in his notebook. With the jury out of the courtroom,
Max Fink made a final, passionate plea to have 'contemporary
community standards' introduced as part of the defence, making a half-hour speech in support of free speech, but the judge
ruled again to deny.

When Max called his witnesses, no one in the jury seemed
to be showing much interest. All experts in censorship and
free speech were disallowed and those who survived the challenge from the bench really had little to say, except that they
hadn't seen Jim expose himself.

There was one other small drama not told until now.
During the trial, the judge went to a restaurant and was ques-
tioned about the case by friends with whom he was dining.

Mike Gershman said, 'A girl overheard the judge say, "Don't worry about it, we're going to throw him in jail," or words to that effect. "We're going to get him." One of the local attorneys found out who the girl was and it turned out she was an entertainer. I was sent to talk to the girl, to see if she would testify about what she overheard in the restaurant, because this was grounds for a mistrial, because the judge cannot go around saying somebody is guilty before the trial's over. She was at the airport on her way to Las Vegas. I rushed to the airport, found her, she said she wasn't interested, didn't want to get involved. I had been told to make a pitch other than money or morality, and what'd that leave? I asked, "Want to meet Jim Morrison?" She said no, got on the plane, and that's the last we saw of her.'

When the verdict was finally read, Jim put down the book he was reading, a biography of Jack London, and looked without emotion at the judge. He had been found guilty of exposure and profanity. On all other charges, including drunkenness, he was found innocent. Bail was set, a date was scheduled for sentencing, and Jim returned to Los Angeles.

Said Mike Gershman, 'The last time we talked was about a book called *The Last Strange Voyage of Donald Crowhurst*, an amazing book. The trial wasn't over and we all knew he was going to be found guilty of something. The book's about a guy in a boat race and he's the first person to travel thousands of miles and reach a set point. Well, Donald Crowhurst decides to take a shortcut, rather than go the prescribed distance, and he alters his log and he wins. But he cracks up because the winning becomes paramount and he does the deceitful thing and is so appalled with himself that he goes stark raving crazy. I knew the book and Jim had just read it. Jim had tremendous empathy for this guy. Jim knew the trial was really over and that his career was really over, no matter what remained to be done.'

In September Jim told Salli Stevenson of *Circus* magazine that the Miami concert was his declaration of independence. The audience was there not to listen to music, but to see him do something outrageous, and he was telling them to wake up. His image had gotten out of hand, he said, and however

responsible he was for that happening, he was 'fed up'. He had lived a couple of lifetimes in just a few years, he added, and if he had to go to jail, he hoped the other three Doors would continue as an instrumental trio. And if he had it to do over, he would do it differently: rather than be the Roman candle, he would go for the 'quiet, demonstrative artist-plodding-in-his-own-garden trip'.

Jim returned to Miami the end of October, just a week before election time. The judge delivered a campaign speech, telling Jim, 'the suggestion that your conduct was acceptable by community standards is just not true. To admit that this nation accepts as a community standard the indecent exposure and the offensive language spoken by you would be to admit that a small minority who spew obscenities, who disregard law and order, and who display utter contempt for our institutions and heritage have determined the community standards for all.'

For exposure and profanity, Jim was given the maximum: a fine of $500 and six months in Raiford Prison, widely recognized as one of the nation's nastiest.

Jim's personal life was equally turbulent. Early in the year, he sent his poetry books to and then started corresponding with Patricia Kennealy, the magazine editor he had met in New York following the Madison Square Garden show. Patricia liked some of the poetry and reviewed it intelligently in her magazine, *Jazz & Pop*. Patricia told me that it was well short of a rave review, but apparently Jim was impressed. He sent her a telegram saying, 'Thanks for the pat on the back' and later told her, 'It was the first time anyone'd reviewed his work and not him.'

The relationship was spotty, like most with Jim (including Pamela's). Their times together were infrequent and rather ordinary; they went to see a couple of movies together (something by Ingmar Bergman; Mick Jagger's *Ned Kelly*), they sat in the lighting booth with Allen Ginsberg to watch the

Jim Morrison and Pamela Courson. Pamela stood
by him to the end.

Jefferson Airplane in concert, they went shopping for books, they went for a walk in Central Park. More unusual, Jim corresponded with Patricia, sending her 'notes on steno pads, four or five pages, one or two words to a line, only four or five lines to a page.

'He said he used to practice his signature a lot,' Patricia said. 'He was proud of it. He'd decided at an early age what it was going to look like, with the "J" and the "M" stuck together. It was very studied.'

Jim was intrigued. The books they bought together revealed a shared intelligence. Jim bought a 'copy of Shakespeare's sonnets, lots of Petrarch, *The Thousand Songs of Mila Rape*, the airplane poems of Allen Ginsberg . . . ' and Patricia gave him a book by Robert Graves called *Watch the North Wind Rise*, 'because he was interested in the occult at that time. I'd just told him I was a witch and he wanted to know everything. I reduced it to its most basic terms. I said it was a pagan mother-worship and he thought that was absolutely terrific, goddess rather than god worship, so I gave him a couple of books to read. '

They made love in June 1970 and were 'married' on June 24th in Patricia's Lower East Side apartment in a witch's ceremony. Standing in candle light before a high priestess of Patricia's coven, they both pricked their hands, dropping blood into a glass of wine, which they then shared. A drop of blood was affixed to the certificate which Jim signed in huge script 'JMorrison'. Patricia said that was when Jim fainted.

About two months later, mid-way through the trial in Miami, Patricia called and then went to Miami, saying she was pregnant and what was Jim going to do? Initially, Jim avoided Patricia, and when he finally agreed to meet her he was, by turns, compassionate, evasive, and coy.

She said, 'I'm sorry, I know it 's a bad time and you're hung up with the trial, but I don't like this any more than you do and it was your fault, you did a dumb thing and pulled out my diaphragm, and we're just gonna have to do something about it.' He acknowledged that the child probably was his, said he didn't want to be a father, or married, offered to pay for an abortion and promised to hold her hand during the operation, and then said, shyly, 'You know, it'd really be an incredible kid.'

Patricia said, 'Yeah, but I don't think that's any reason to have the kid. You just don't see if two terrific people can turn out a terrific product together. You don't really care for kids that much in the first place. What'd I do with it? I mean, the only reason I'd have it would be because it was yours, and I don't think that's any reason to have the child.'

Jim said, 'You know, this subject has never come up before.'

Patricia said, 'Don't give me that bullshit, I know it has.'

He said, 'No, no, never. This is the first time.'

Patricia decided to hell with it and they went off to the hotel bar and got drunk.

Jim was not present in November when Patricia had her abortion. By then he was in a tailspin. Billy Siddons and the Doors' agents were lining up fewer and fewer concerts and on top of that, it continued difficult to get Jim into a studio to record new material. That was one of the reasons for assembling *Absolutely Live*, the double album that was recorded over a period of more than six months and released in July. Live albums had been successful for several bands in 1969 and it was regarded as an easy way for a band to satisfy a contractual obligation to produce an agreed-upon number of albums in an agreed length of time. In the Doors' case, it also took up the slack in unfertile times.

Paul Rothchild, the producer who had been with the Doors from the start, hated the album. He said, 'It shouldn't have been made and shouldn't have been released. It should have been made as a movie. It was difficult to convey the Doors live on tape. The Doors' albums were overstatement from the very first, in much the same way that a Shakespearean actor must overstate his lines to reach the back of the theatre. You couldn't do a straight recording of the Doors and succeed after the first album. It required a ten to one ratio, which is a low recovery average.

'The Doors were not great live performers musically. They were exciting theatrically and kinetically, but as musicians they didn't make it, there was too much inconsistency, there was too much bad music. Robby would be horrendously out of tune with Ray, John would be missing cues, there was bad mike usage too where you couldn't hear Jim at all. As a movie it still would've worked.

'It shouldn't have been released because live albums were a drug on the market by then. The public had tired of them. But the general consensus in the industry among the top people was live LPs were a great way to catch another album from a group having a slow time recording and to catch the peak of a buying wave. It was logical, but the music market didn't go for it. Jac Holzman even insisted the album sell for $11.90 – the equivalent of two $5.95 records. We were hoping at the worst it'd sell for $6.95 and then wouldn't be a drug on the market. It turned out to be the worst disaster the Doors ever had, saleswise.'

When more time went by without any promise of new material, Elektra Records began planning its first repackaging of old hits, which became 13, a collection of thirteen previously recorded songs, including all the hits. (The official line at Elektra was that there were thirteen songs because the most anyone included on an album during this period was twelve – with the number declining fast – and, thus, thirteen was a bargain. Others said that the title was connected to the highly publicized fact that the thirteenth letter in the alphabet was M, which stood for Marijuana. As bizarre as this argument may sound today, it was not strange in 1970; many record buyers wore an 'M' or '13' patch on their jackets.) The record was released in November, the same month Patricia had her abortion.

By now, Pam was heavily into heroin. At first, she merely toyed with it, when it was offered by some of her one-night dates. Now there were binges. Eve Babitz, who had taken Jim to bed when the group was just getting started and now eaked out a living designing album covers, remained a part of the same L.A. rock scene; her sister had made some of Jim's leather suits and Eve drank in the same bars with Jim. Eve said about Pam, 'Everything a nerd could possibly wish to be, Pamela was. She had drugs, took heroin, and was fearless in every situation. Socially she didn't care, emotionally she was shockproof, and as for her eating disorders – her idea of the

Jim and Pam with their dog, Sage.

diet to be on while Jim was in Miami going to court was ten days of heroin. Every time she awoke she did some, so she just sort of slept through her fast.'

Jim was back to drugs as well. Jim had gotten involved with the wife of a film maker he had met while making *HWY*. Call her Magda. The publisher of *No One Here Gets Out Alive* changed her name for legal reasons and I'll change it again. It doesn't matter. Magda was one of Jim's cocaine girls.

Jim started using coke early in the year, during the period when he was meeting with MGM and writing his screenplay with Michael McClure. At one point he gave one of his film contacts an ounce of the stuff and told him to hold on to it and not to give him more than a gram at a time, no matter what he said. Jim loved coke in the same way he enjoyed his earlier drugs, and he went at it in the same unbridled manner. Echoing a famous mountain climber's reason for scaling Mount Everest, he told a friend, 'If there was a mountain of coke in the yard I'd do it up . . . because it was there.'

'I never had coke before,' Magda told me. 'I was a hyped-up person anyway and on coke, watch out! He liked that. He knew when my husband was going to Mexico and at eleven that night the doorbell rang.

'"Who is it?'

'"Jimmy."

'"Which Jimmy?" I opened the door a crack and he put his foot in so I couldn't close it.

'We really got it on. Neither of us was expecting it. He really loved life, and so did I. The only bad thing was there was too much cocaine, which blew our minds. He was trying to live a hundred years in one – going to restaurants and ordering all kinds of food, like for ten people and eating a little bit of everything, or nothing at all. He wanted to try everything, I guess. He thought I was crazier than he was and he wanted to see how far I'd go. And he supplied the coke, a jar of it, with champagne and stuff. And we'd get more crazy and crazy every day until one day there was this really frightening scene.

'One evening he came home and he had all this coke and we had almost all of it and all the champagne and everything.

He learned that I freak out real bad . . . I like to have . . . sometimes, I, you know, drink blood, for instance . . . being from Transylvania. And he said, "Well, why don't we drink some blood?"

'I got some dirty razor blades and cut myself. He didn't dare to cut himself because he was scared of any pain. So I started cutting away, all these cuts. Because the blood didn't come at first.'

Magda showed me the backs of her hands. There were eight or ten half-inch scars on each, at the base of her thumbs.

'And suddenly it came and we just had blood all over the place and freaked out and danced in the moonshine,' she said. 'Just wheeeeeewwww-eeee-ooooooo. And after that we just got very scared where it can go, you know, because the mornings after these freakouts are really sad. Waking up and all these pools of blood . . . '

Jim had moved into the Château Marmont, the hotel where, years later, John Belushi overdosed. In 1970, it was still known mainly as a temporary home for visiting actors from New York, but the rock and rollers were making it their home, as well. I visited there earlier in the year to interview the singer-songwriter Tim Hardin. Jim came by the same day and sat quietly against a wall for several hours, just watching the scene. Tim, who was a heroin addict, went into the bathroom at some point and shot up, leaving the sink and mirror and wall splattered with his blood for all to see. When Jim moved into one of the cottages near the pool at the end of 1970, the hotel's reputation was still going down.

A film writer named Larry Marcus visited him there several times. He had presented a story line to Jim during the Miami trial about a rock singer who'd committed a 'public disgrace at the Albert Hall in London'. Marcus said it was based on Jim's own story and, predictably, Jim hated the idea.

Over the next six months they discussed several other ideas. 'We came up with a motherfucker of an idea, a marvellous film that we had to do, with a human being who wanted to vanish from the world and become zero,' Marcus said. 'The hero was to have nothing to do with music. He insisted upon that. The hero he most liked was a Los Angeles film editor.

149

The suggestion of doing anything about Jim as a singer was over, to his great relief, because he could then put so much of himself into the character who was not a singer, and as he talked about that character, it was Jim again. It was Jim who was married and had kids and left it all behind because in his desperate search – in his frantic search for zero. Those were Jim's exact words: "frantic search for zero." The film editor went to Mexico for a few days and kept on going. Ultimately the man was in a jungle in which no one else lived, alone. I had a feeling that was a very crucial metaphor for how he felt about himself.

'I got money for the film – like that!' Marcus snapped his fingers. 'From Fred Weintraub, who had produced a couple of films at that time, including *Woodstock*. All Fred wanted was absolute living proof that Jim would do the film and he'd go with the money. We were going to co-write, co-produce, and co-direct, Jim and Larry . . . '

It ended badly one night when Marcus and Frank Lisciandro and Jim went to dinner on the Sunset Strip. Jim drank an entire bottle of scotch and verbally destroyed Marcus's story line, ridiculing it, and him, just before going out onto Sunset Boulevard to direct traffic with his coat as if the passing BMWs and Corvettes were bulls.

Soon after that, on his 27th birthday, December 8th, Jim said he wanted to record some of his poetry. The engineer who had worked his early recordings with the Doors, John Haeny, booked Village Recorders in West Los Angeles, near the bar where Jim had done much of his heavy drinking during his days at UCLA. Haeny brought a bottle of Bushmill's Irish whisky and gave it to Jim. Jim drank it as he read his poetry. Haeny walked away at the end of the evening with six hours of tape, most of it unusable because of Jim's drunkenness. Jim's friends, who had accompanied him to the studio, walked away with Jim unconscious, carrying him by his arms and legs.

Haeny told me he had, maybe, eighty minutes of usable poetry and with that, he signed a letter of agreement with Jim the last day of December 1970 to produce an album of poetry, to be released by Elektra.

At the same time, Jim and the other Doors decided to record what became their final album together. Though the band had been through hard times, rarely working together and talking together only a little more, they had managed to plan some songs. Jim brought in some poetry and they worked together in the rehearsal studio, set up in the ground floor room of the Doors office building.

The band played the songs for Paul Rothchild, who hated them. 'It was awful,' he told me. 'The material was bad, the attitude was bad, the performance was bad. After three days of listening, I said, "That's it!" on the talk-back, cancelled the session, went in and talked to them for three straight hours.

'I said, "Look, I think it sucks, I don't think the world wants to hear it, it's the first time I've ever been bored in a recording studio in my life, I want to go to sleep. The tensions between you guys are phenomenal." I said, "Jim, this is your record. This is the record you have wanted, so you got to get it together. Why don't you guys produce it yourself? I'm gonna drop out." They all came to rely on me getting it to happen so much that I'd found myself becoming more of a cop than a producer. I won't do that in a studio. If the lead singer doesn't want to show up for a session, I don't either.'

The Doors were disappointed and angry, but they believed in the material and decided to take Paul's advice and record the songs themselves. They asked Bruce Botnick, their old engineer, to assist and all agreed to use the Doors' rehearsal room as the studio and the small rest room upstairs as the vocal booth. The result was *L.A. Woman*, an album that was regarded, critically, as one of their two or three best.

One of the longest and ultimately most popular songs on the album was 'Riders On The Storm', a song that started out with the sound of rainfall. Paul Rothchild thought it sounded like 'cocktail lounge music' – at the time, many chi-chi cocktail lounges had fake thunderstorms and the sound of rain as part of the backdrop to the martinis served – and he was equally disparaging about the song that was released as the first single from the album, 'Love Her Madly,' a typical Doors love song.

This does the album an injustice. 'Riders On The Storm' was one of the best tracks, in fact; despite some terrible imagery and banal rhyming, it still managed to be compelling. Arguably the best track was the title song, 'L.A. Woman', Jim's farewell to Los Angeles. And, reminiscent of some earlier blues covers, Jim sang 'Crawling King Snake,' a classic by John Lee Hooker.

More than ever, Jim was walking the streets of West Los Angeles, a hulking, overweight man, bearded, wearing jeans and a rumpled Army fatigue jacket, walking, walking, walking, as if trying to burn the images of the tarnished neighbourhood between Sunset and Santa Monica Boulevards indelibly into his whisky and beer-soaked brain.

Past the Doors' office and the Elektra studios. Past the building where Pamela had her unsuccessful boutique and he had his unproductive film offices. Past the Phone Booth and the Palms and Barney's and all the other cheap bars where he usually stopped for a while to drink. Past Jerry Lewis' and Dean Martin's old clubs and the Playboy Club and the Body Shop (a strip joint) on the Sunset Strip. Past the fashion showroom on Santa Monica Boulevard where Rudi Gernriech designed and introduced the topless bathing suit. Past motorcycle shops and antique stores and every kind of restaurant you can imagine. Past the hundreds of low-rise, stucco apartment buildings, anonymously lined up behind thirsty-looking palm trees, looking tired in the constant smog.

Jim and Pamela still lived on the second floor in one of those apartment buildings, on Norton Avenue, and Diane Gardiner remained downstairs. Between them, and their weird friends, it was like a strange situation comedy, of the sort that David Lynch would like, or maybe Martin Scorcese. Jim was still throwing his books out of the window during evening fights and collecting them in the morning.

Patricia Kennealy told me that in December, 1970, about a month after the abortion, she flew to Los Angeles and left a message at the Doors' office for Jim, fastened to his desk with

Jim on stage in January 1970 at the Felt Forum, a
concert hall attached to Madison Square Garden,
New York.

a knife. She then moved into Diane's apartment. 'Jim called half an hour later,' Patricia said. 'Pam was upstairs at the time. The Doors were recording [*L.A. Woman*] and he asked me to the session. I said recording sessions bore me, why not come here? He said okay and didn't show. I didn't hear from him for three or four days.

'I was at home alone, the phone rings, and it's some girl calling for Pam. Jim and Pam didn't have a phone. So I got Pam and I said, "I met you once, at the Hilton in New York, we had dinner with some other people." Pam was really stoned and she said, "Yeah, whatever happened to that chick, Pat Kennedy . . . Pat Connolly . . . ?" I said, "Pamela, that's me." We talked for three hours, we got stoned and drunk and things got said. There were no ill feelings. It was very lovely and very weird. She told me she wasn't married to Jim and I told her about the baby. I didn't really want to hurt her, but we were smashed and everything just came out. We'd had six joints.

'She said, "Oh, wow, that's so beautiful, but it would've been more beautiful if you could've loved Jim enough to have the baby." That pissed me off. I said, "I loved Jim and I love myself and I loved the kid enough not to have the baby, you know." She said, "Yeah, but if you'd a had the kid, you could a gone away and lived in the country. Of course Jim never would a sent you any money, because that's the way he is . . . "'

At this point, Jim came up the walk. Pamela went 'dead white and rushed out to Jim, pleading, "Jim, Jim, don't look in there . . . it's only Diane."'

Jim laughed and entered the apartment and after a while, and some wine, they started playing the card game War. Jim won the first fifteen or twenty hands and after a while Pamela tried to get Jim to go upstairs with her. He refused.

'Finally, Diane gave Pamela some amyl nitrate and took her upstairs,' Patricia said. 'Jim had a room at the Château and he said he wanted to go there. Then he changed his mind and said he was too drunk to drive, he wanted to stay there. I said, "Here? Where are we going to sleep? On the floor?" He said, "Yeah," and started taking his clothes off. I got a quilt off

Diane's bed and wrapped us up in it and we went to sleep.

'At ten the next morning, Pamela came downstairs, and came to the door. I was cringing. Diane came out of the bedroom, opened the door, said, "I'm not gonna deny he's here." Pamela came in, stood over us. It was like some bad French bedroom farce. It was so ludicrous, so horrible and so funny all at once, no one knew whether to laugh or cry or kill each other.

'Pamela said, "I have only one thing to say to you and I'm gonna say it in front of all these people: 'Jim, you've ruined my Christmas. You spoil it for me every year. This is the fourth year. I just can't stand it any more."

'I said, "Pamela, it isn't what it seems to be, it's perfectly innocent, let me explain . . . "

'And Diane says, "Pamela, what you need is some vitamin pills and some orange juice, come out to the kitchen with me and . . . come on, come on." We get up and Jim's bitching, "Oh, my god, I'll never hear the end of this." I said, "Jim, you wanted it to happen. It was your idea to stay here." He said, "Yeah, yeah, you're always right."

'Pamela came out of the kitchen and we all sat around drinking more wine. I finally reached over and put my arm around her and said, "Pamela, it's all in the family, don't worry about it".

'A month later Patricia paid another visit to California, staying this time with other friends into February, when a major earthquake hit Los Angeles. 'I was panicked, frightened to death,' Patricia told me. 'There were predictions of the city's doom. A full moon. An eclipse. It was all happening that Thursday night. I went to a recording session with my girlfriend with whom I had been staying and she made a play for Jim. I said, "Oh, that's a no-no, wait until I leave. I don't care what you do, but not in front of me, please."

'Because I didn't care what Jim did. He was the complete polygamist. But she was really drunk and Jim was easily lured away. She went to the john and five minutes later Jim left. I found them embracing outside on the lawn. I walked over and said, "Get up!" Jim was smiling, he thought it was funny. I said, "Come on up, both of you, up!"

'So the girl reaches up and pulls me down. My inclination is somewhere between group grope and mayhem. I said, "Let me talk to him by myself." She went away.

'And he said, "Listen, you know I'm too drunk to screw tonight, just let me sleep with her."

'I said, "Look, it's my last night in L.A., I'm going home tomorrow and I'll probably never see you again . . . "

'He said, "Well, I'm not gonna spend another night with you."

'I said, "Okay with me, but you're damned well not going to spend it with her, either." He got disgusted and went inside and she came over and I said, "I'm gonna break your fucking neck." She said, "Don't hurt me, don't hurt me, it's not my fault." Then we went to a topless place, the Phone Booth, where Jim tells her I'm a frustrated lesbian and I go bananas, absolutely bananas.

'We went back to her house and and had a scene in the bath-room where I told her to cool it and she said, "Well, you've always known how fond I was of him." I said, "You fuck, you always told me it was Kris Kristofferson you were after." She pushed me backward and I fell into the bathtub. I got out of the tub, grabbed her by her hair and slammed her into the side of the sink and was going for her eyes when Morrison came in, saying, "Nowwwwwwww, ladies . . . "

'We left the bathroom and Jim started going through all the drawers in the apartment. We asked him what he was looking for and he said, "Oh, I'm looking for knives and scissors, so you can't castrate me." We were flabbergasted, we didn't know what to do, so we watched him gather up all the sharp things in the house and put them under the couch. Then he laid on the couch and said he didn't think he had anything to do with the whole thing, he said he thought it was between us two. And then he passed out.

'She suggested we go outside to talk, so we wouldn't wake him up, then proposed we share him, so we could keep him from the groupies and those who didn't really care for him. I saw red. I've never been that angry. It was like looking through red cellophane. I screamed, "YOU FUCKING BITCH, I'M GOING TO KILL YOU!" I grabbed her, threw her down the stairs, gave her a couple of punches, threw her up against the wall, and she said, "I don't want to fight you . . . "

'I said, "FIGHT, YOU FUCKING CUNT OR I'LL KILL YOU!" So she gave me a powderpuff punch and I went into a real rage, giving her a karate number with my foot in her stomach, then I started punching her in the face, and finally I went away, just like that. It was over and I was drained. I told her to take me to the airport and I got on a plane to New York that morning.'

I've devoted far more space to this incident that it deserves, except that it was typical. This is what Jim's life was like, and had been like, from the time he left UCLA through his final days in Los Angeles four years later. I didn't see him much during this period. Occasionally we'd run into each other at one of the bars. But I heard from mutual friends about various scenes that weren't all that different from this one. He was rolling along, drunk much of the time, putting himself out there, pretty much letting life happen to him.

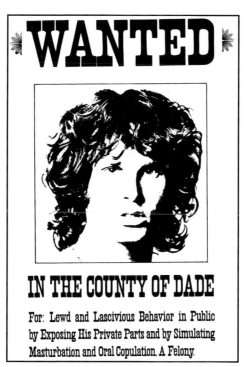

WANTED

IN THE COUNTY OF DADE

For: Lewd and Lascivious Behavior in Public by Exposing His Private Parts and by Simulating Masturbation and Oral Copulation. A Felony.

VI

THE EXILE

PAM WAS THE FIRST to talk about Paris. According to Diane Gardiner, she fell in love with a French count, variously identified as Jaime de Bretaille and Jean DeBretti. For more than a year, they had been sharing heroin along with fantasies.

'Pam was fascinated by the idea of royalty,' Diane told me. 'Now, I don't know if he really was a count, but Pam and Jim were fighting and she told me, "The time has come. I've outgrown Jim and it's time to move on. I have this French count who is just dying to be with me." She talked about him all the time. He was so very rich. He and his friends were terribly bored and they took a lot of heroin. He'd tell her, "We're the last of the dinosaurs" – the aristocracy was dying out.'

Jim showed an interest in Paris as well. Some of his friends had lived there and they shared with him their love of the city. After all these years, Jim remained enamoured of many French poets and novelists. With its long, rich tradition of literary exiles, it seemed to offer Jim a comfortable escape hatch, a refuge, a place in which to relax and regroup.

Pam left California first and Jim followed, after spending a few days with Babe. As I look back, I think Babe probably was Jim's closest friend, perhaps the only one who accepted Jim unconditionally, who wanted nothing in return. They shot pool on the Strip and went to Catalina in a boat the Doors had purchased. They went to the Muhammed Ali-Joe Frazier fight. They drank. Jim flew to Paris in early March.

At first, Paris seemed to deliver what Jim wanted, or at least a huge chunk of it. After spending a couple of weeks in a small hotel, they subleased a large, airy apartment in a nice district near the Bastille and in the weeks following Jim wandered the

159

city, visiting museums, tracking down the homes and haunts of his literary heroes, stopping at the sidewalk cafés. Jim and Pam – whose count by now had left Paris – drove to the south of France and into Spain, then took a ship to Tangier, where they rented another car and drove to Casablanca. Another time, they spent a week in Corsica. Jim went to the theatre. He developed a friendship with two French film makers, Agnes Varda and her husband Jacques Demy. (Demy was best known outside France for directing *Umbrellas of Cherbourg* and she was acknowledged as the 'grandmother of New Wave cinema'.) Jim shaved off his beard and lost some weight. He started wearing khaki slacks and crew-neck sweaters, looking very much like an ageing college student. For four months, there were no major incidents.

There were, of course, many small ones. Despite what Pam would say later, Jim continued to drink heavily. In Los Angeles, Jim sometimes had to walk for a few blocks between bars; in Paris, the romantic bistros and sidewalk cafés were everywhere. Paris also offered some sleazy rock and roll clubs of the sort he had loved in Los Angeles. Frequently, Jim found himself going home with people he met along the way. Often, he was drunk for days at a time.

Friends told me that when he called California – rarely – and was told that the critics loved the new album and that it was selling well, he was excited. He told John Densmore that he was writing again and the material was the best he'd ever done – apparently a lie, based on what others said and entries in a fragmentary journal he had begun to keep. He told some of the people he met in Paris that he was writing an opera. The truth is, he spent hours sitting with his notebooks open in front of him, staring for hours at the blank page without writing a word.

Jim tried 'automatic writing', letting his mind empty, hoping that something would be created freely and spontaneously. He tried discipline, sitting down at the desk each day at the same time. He actually hired a secretary, a young American, Robin Wertle, who was fluent in French. Nothing worked.

He got depressed. Enormously depressed, said one friend who saw him in the the final days. By mid-June 1971, his

French friend from Los Angeles, Alain Ronay, was living in the flat with Jim and Pam. At the end of the month he moved into the home of Agnes Varda and Jacques Demy, but stayed in touch. Years later, Ronay revealed that on July 2nd he spent much of the day with Jim. They took a walk, he said, and Jim was attacked with a fit of hiccuping that continued for nearly an hour. Ronay said Jim didn't look well and he told him so. Jim rarely complained and shrugged it off, saying he felt fine. But Ronay said that at the end of the walk, Jim had difficulty breathing when they carried firewood up to the apartment from the building's courtyard. Before leaving, Ronay recommended that they attend a screening that night of *Pursued*, an offbeat American western starring Robert Mitchum. Pam the next day told police they had seen a film called *Death Valley*.

What happened following the movie was, for a long time, open to conjecture – the subject of wild disagreement and controversy.

I was living in London in 1972, the following year, and I visited Paris several times in my search for information. The stories I was told about Jim's death were confusing. The one I heard most often was that Jim died from an overdose of heroin in a nightclub called the Rock'n'Roll Circus. This is a version I heard repeatedly during my interviews and later was confirmed by sources in the junkie underground talking to Hervé Muller, a French journalist who picked up some of the threads of the story after I returned to the U.S.

Junkies are generally not known for their reliability. Usually they are anxious to say anything they think the listener wants to hear, in exchange, they hope, for enough money to score another bag of relief. None of the sources with whom Hervé talked was paid for information beyond the cost of coffee at some sidewalk cafe. Nor was any 'ulterior' motive apparent, at least to Hervé or me. Junkies generally don't look for publicity and there is little status to be gained amongst other junkies, or anyone else, to say you shared heroin with Jim Morrison the night he died of an overdose.

Of course, there's always a chance that some nut made up the whole story and that it started going around, building up, becoming more elaborate as it travelled. But the lack of contradiction on the basic points of the story is impressive.

Nor does it seem that this version of Jim's death was a fabrication created to counter the 'official' version. To the contrary, the 'official' version – death by a heart attack in a bathtub – seemed totally unknown in the junkie underground until its members were interviewed.

Jim was familiar with the junkie underground, or at least aware of it, not because of Pamela's sporadic use of the drug, but because of the dives in which he chose to drink. The most notable of these in Paris at the time was the Circus, where the walls were covered with huge photographs of rock stars wearing clown costumes. Earlier, this was the slickest rock club in Paris – where Led Zeppelin, Richie Havens, and Johnny Winter had played – but by Summer 1971, it had slid close to the bottom. Rock and roll was still the music played, but now most of the action wasn't on the dance floor, it was in the toilets. Occasionally the place was raided by police and that would precipitate an exodus that related to the junkies' version of Jim's death.

The Circus was situated at 57 rue de Seine, on the Left Bank near the river, and it backed up to a much more respectable club, called the Alcazar. The Alcazar, at 62 rue Mazarine, presented an expensive dinner-spectacle of French music and scantily clad dancers, catering to a crowd of middle-aged French businessmen. The club was large, seating close to a thousand patrons on three levels, surrounding a stage about four times the size of that of the more famous Latin Quarter. For some of the junkies in the Circus, when police arrived, the escape route was through the Circus kitchen, which had a back door leading into the Alcazar's kitchen. It was a simple matter then to slip from the kitchen through the darkened club and onto the adjoining street without being noticed.

According to information gathered by Hervé Muller, one of the dealers on the scene in the summer of 1971 was a Chinese called 'Le Chinoise'. Supposedly, he had a laboratory for making heroin in Marseille, which explains why he happened to

Jim 'in hiding' in a Paris cafe. He left America
full of plans for a new beginning.

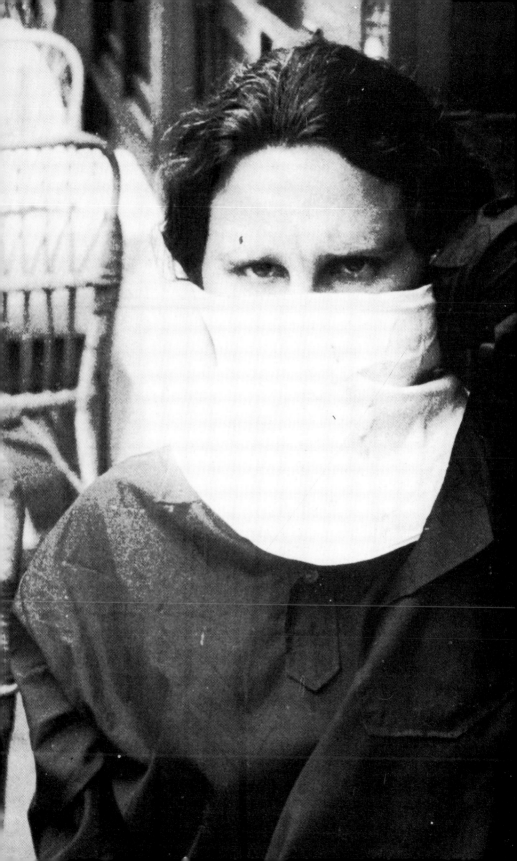

have such unusually potent heroin to sell, running to about 30 per cent 'pure' instead of the customary 5 to 10 per cent. The way the story goes, 'Le Chinoise', who was not known to use heroin himself, sold a quantity to a second-level dealer named Michel, who in turn sold a smaller quantity to someone called 'Le Petit Bernard', charging him $100. Bernard then sold that packet to Jim for about $200, warning him of the potency.

'That's okay,' Jim reportedly said, 'I'm used to it.' All sources say Jim seemed to be nervous, upset.

All sources also told Hervé Muller that the final transaction took place in the men's room of the Circus, where Jim snorted the heroin, then slumped into a comatose state. The junkies present heaved him to his feet between them, guiding him back into the night club, then through the adjoining kitchens to the Alcazar, and into a cab on the street.

At this point, it is generally agreed that Jim was still alive. This is reasonable. In most heroin overdoses, the victim generally dies after one or two hours of lethargy, stupor, and coma. The way this story ends, Jim was returned to his flat and dumped into a bathtub full of cold water in an attempt to revive him, standard treatment for an overdose, although there is some question about its practicality. That was one version of how Jim died. Of course it wasn't the only one.

In a second, far more innocent story, outlined in a statement given to Paris police the day Jim died, and thereafter described as The Official Version of the Death, Pam said that she and Jim returned to the flat from the movie theatre about 1am and after she washed some dishes and Jim watched some home movies projected on the apartment wall, they went to bed, falling asleep about 2.30am while listening to some records.

About an hour later, Pam told police (in a deposition taken several hours after Jim died), she was awakened by Jim's noisy breathing. She said she wasn't sure of the time, because there was no clock in the bedroom. She thought Jim might be suffocating and shook him. He didn't wake up. She slapped him a few times and then shook him again. Finally, he opened his eyes. He told Pam that he wasn't feeling well and after pacing in the bedroom for a minute or two, told Pam that he wanted to take a warm bath.

Once in the tub, Pam told police, Jim said he felt nauseous. Pam brought an orange cooking pot from the kitchen and Jim vomited. Pam cleaned the pot in the nearby sink and Jim threw up a second time, expelling a quantity of blood. Again Pam cleaned the pot and a third time Jim vomited, now a few blood clots. She told police that Jim insisted 'it's over'; he was feeling better and he didn't want her to call a doctor. Pam quoted Jim as saying he would finish his bath and he urged Pam to return to bed. She said colour had returned to his face and she felt 'reassured', so she did as he suggested, falling asleep.

Pam said she 'awoke with a start' some time later and saw that she was in bed alone. She got up and went to the bathroom, where she found Jim still in the bath. His eyes were closed and he was smiling, she said, his head tilted back on the edge of the tub, turned to one side. Pam said she thought he was joking and, according to Diane Gardiner, she stood there talking to him for some time. She told him it was a dumb joke. She said she knew what he was doing; he was trying to scare her. Slowly, Pam did become scared. She noticed there was some blood under one nostril. She shook him.

She told police she thought she could awaken him. She tried to get him out of the tub and couldn't. That was when, panicked because she couldn't speak French and telephone for help, she called Alain Ronay at Agnes Varda's house. Years later, Varda said that the call came about 8am, an hour at which she never answered the telephone. But Ronay picked up the receiver and heard Pam say, 'I can't wake him up. I think he's dying.' Ronay went to Varda's room, woke her, and she called for an ambulance immediately. Ronay wrote out the Morrison address as Varda dialled the emergency number for the fire brigade. Ronay hurriedly told her not to reveal Jim's celebrity and when the telephone conversation was completed, they drove to the Morrison apartment.

In interviews she and Ronay gave to *Paris Match* in 1991, both he and Varda say that when they arrived, they saw firemen on the street. Ronay asked, 'Is he okay?' and was told to ask his questions upstairs. Ronay and Varda went up to the second floor appartment.

Jim and Pam in Paris shortly before Jim's
untimely death in July, 1971.

The Exile

There is a contradiction in the Ronay and Varda stories at this point. Varda remembers clearly that when they arrived, Jim was still in the tub, surrounded by members of the fire brigade. On the other hand, Ronay says that Jim was already on the bed and that he never saw the body. Varda's accurate description of the death scene in the bathroom gives credence to her story over Ronay's.

Fire Lt. Alain Raisson said in his statement to police that he and his men responded to a call of 'asphyxie', or asphyxiation, and were greeted by a 'young woman who could not speak French'. This was Pamela, who led them to the bathroom where they found 'a man in the bath, completely naked and heavily built. His head was above the water, reclining to one side on the edge of the bath. The bath was full of water, pinkish in colour, and his right arm was resting on the side of the bath.' Both the water and the body were described as 'lukewarm'.

With his men, Raisson removed the body from the tub and carried it into the bedroom, where they placed it on the floor and attempted cardio-pulmonary resuscitation. Raisson said a quantity of blood ran from Jim's right nostril when they laid him down. When it was clear that Jim was dead, Raisson had his men move the body to the bed.

A second report was filed the same day by Jacques Manchez, a police officer who arrived to find Jim covered by a spread on the bed. He noted blood running from one nostril, a clot closing the other one, and ordered the spread pulled back. He then searched for any signs of 'trauma', such as wounds or needle marks, and found none. He also reported that there were no signs of 'disorder' in the room (evidence of a fight).

When Ronay and Varda entered the apartment they went directly to Pam, who was wearing a white robe she had bought in Algiers. She merely said Jim was dead. Before they could talk further, the police arrived, with Jacques Manchez in charge. In an effort to cloak the death in further mystery, Ronay and Pam told the officer that Jim's name was Douglas James Morrison, transposing the first and middle names. They also identified Jim merely as a poet. Manchez was suspicious, asking, 'How could Jim be a poet? He was so young.'

Ronay said, 'Was Victor Hugo born with a white beard? Did Rimbaud have one when he died?'

Manchez asked how a mere poet could have afforded such a spacious apartment in such a good neighbourhood.

Ronay said Jim was independently wealthy.

Their conversation was interrupted by the arrival of Dr. Max Vassille, a physician on the staff of the Paris Medical University. He was called by the office of Police Superintendent Robert Berry in accordance with the penal procedures code. Manchez told Ronay that the doctor's findings would determine whether or not the police would open an investigation into the death.

Ronay asked what sort of investigation he was talking about. Manchez said that if the doctor found anything out of order, many officers would be involved.

When Dr. Vassille emerged from the bedroom, he asked Pam if Jim used drugs. Ronay answered for her. He said Jim drank, but never used drugs; he never even smoked marijuana in Los Angeles, where it was as freely available as cigarettes.

The doctor's official statement filed later that day ruled that death was due to natural causes. He noted the blood around the nostrils, but said there were no signs of trauma (wounds, puncture marks). Vassille also referred to a conversation he apparently had with Ronay, who said Jim had experienced chest pains for a period of time. The doctor conjectured that there were coronary problems, aggravated by 'abusive drinking'. The change in temperature represented by the warm bath then pushed Jim over the edge, resulting in 'myocardial infarction' – a heart attack.

While the doctor made his examination, the telephone rang. It was Pamela's friend, the Count. Pam took the phone into another room and told her friend that Jim was dead. The Count was with the British pop star Marianne Faithfull at the time of the call, a fact that, later, would explain how the story of Jim's death began to leak out. Apparently, Pam never told anyone what she and the Count said and the Count died a few years later of a heroin overdose.

After hanging up the phone, Pam returned to Ronay and

Varda, taking Ronay's arm. Ronay said, 'Tell me, quickly, how he died.' Pam told him. Ronay and Varda agreed that they had to keep it quiet.

At 3.40 that afternoon, Ronay and Pam went to police head-quarters and gave their depositions, required before the case could be closed. Pam went first – with Ronay translating for her – telling Officer Manchez that shortly after she and Jim had come to Paris, while living in the Hotel de Nice, before moving into the apartment, Jim had a breathing problem, accompanied by a chronic cough. She called a doctor, who came to the hotel and prescribed a medicine normally used by asthmatics. Pam said she couldn't remember the doctor's name and the medicine was thrown away. She added that Jim didn't like doctors and never took care of himself.

In his statement, Ronay gave the police more testimony regarding Jim's poor health. He said, 'I'm sure that my friend didn't take any drugs. He often talked about the stupidity of young people taking drugs. He thought this problem was extremely serious.' He then told the story of his walk with Jim the previous day, when Jim had had an 'attack of hiccups' and had trouble carrying firewood from the courtyard to the flat.

The following day, Police Superintendent Robert Berry filed the last official report, summarizing the statements of the fire brigade, the local police precinct, Dr. Vassille, Pamela, and Ronay. This was a formality required in the filing of a burial certificate, part of closing the case.

'Nothing suspicious was noticed on the spot either in the apartment or on the body, which bore no trace of blows, lesions, or needle marks,' Berry wrote. With no signs of 'foul play', no autopsy was required and Pam was given permission to proceed with the funeral arrangements.

Before I tell what I believe really happened, let me explain why *No One Here Gets Out Alive* ended so ambiguously, hinting strongly that Jim might have engineered a hoax and was still alive. At the time I wrote the book, I really wasn't sure how Jim died, although I was satisfied that he was dead. When Hervé Muller presented the Rock'n'Roll Circus scenario, somehow I doubted it. (Although, to this day, Hervé stands by the story.) It just didn't feel right and of all the variations in Pam's story which emerged once she was back in the United States and confiding in friends, none ever mentioned the Circus or this band of mysterious junkies.

While writing *No One Here*, I was also picking up other theories, right, left, and sideways. Jim had been stabbed to death, or killed by someone sticking pins in a voodoo doll. One story had his death part of a serpentine conspiracy connecting the deaths of John Kennedy, Robert Kennedy, Martin Luther King, Jimi Hendrix, Janis Joplin, the Kent State Five, and several Black Panthers. Each was more ridiculous than the last.

I had to finish the book. I didn't believe the official story for a minute and I didn't feel comfortable with Hervé Muller's carefully researched nightclub toilet overdose. So I reported the many scenarios, a long list that included the possibility that Jim wasn't dead at all, but merely living out an elaborately conceived and brilliantly executed hoax. I believed that this was something that, with Pamela's help, Jim could have pulled off.

Certainly it was something he could have conceived. In college he had explored, intellectually, the possibility that Jesus Christ's death was a hoax. Jim also had joked about faking his own death even before the band had its first hit record. In his interview with me for *Rolling Stone*, Jim talked about the possibility that at some time in the future he could appear with a different identity, wearing a suit and tie. With a Hollywood screenwriter he had devised a plot about someone who disappeared into the jungle in search of 'absolute zero'.

I decided to write two last chapters, one of which had Jim dying of an overdose, the other having him disappear into North Africa, much like his hero, the poet Arthur Rimbaud. I suggested to the publisher that if, say, 10,000 copies of the book were published, 5,000 should end with an overdose caused by the combination of alcohol and heroin, the other 5,000 with the hoax. I asked that the books then be distributed randomly and without comment; let the readers discover the

Jim in a Paris cafe. He shaved off his beard, lost weight, but the dream soon faded.

different endings on their own. I still think it was a good idea, but the publisher disagreed, so *No One Here Gets Out Alive* ended ambiguously, with both final chapters blended into one, leaving the reader uncertain. Of course this served the original purpose, fanning the flames of the rumour that Jim was not dead, but alive somewhere.

The years passed and while I remained convinced that Jim was dead, I still didn't know what happened. At the same time, I came to believe that I might have neglected, or at least underestimated and misunderstood, Pamela's role in Jim's life, and I began to consider writing a second, smaller book, or perhaps a screenplay, focusing on their romance.

I re-interviewed some of my earlier subjects, among them Diane Gardiner. After Jim was buried and when Pam returned to the U.S., Pam moved into Diane's cottage in Sausalito, California. Diane, who was then working as a publicist for the Jefferson Airplane, had been one of Pam's closest confidantes in Los Angeles and I figured that if anyone knew what happened, or at least knew what Pam said happened, it was Diane.

Diane apologized for not telling me more in interviews she gave me when I was researching *No One Here Gets Out Alive*. She said she promised Pamela not to reveal anything about Jim's death and at the time, Pam was still alive, so Diane said she felt bound to her pledge. Now – ten years after Jim's death – Diane told me that when Pam returned from Europe 'she was a real case, just devastated'. Diane said that for several months Pam walked around talking to herself, rambling and making no sense, and when she did make sense, she blamed herself for Jim's death.

'I've never seen anyone feeling so guilty,' Diane told me. 'She had tried to devote her whole life to one person. That was it. That was her life. Her whole life was him. And to have that kicked out from under you...'

As Diane and Pam spent more time together, fragments of the story came together, forming a believable scenario, explaining the source of Pam's guilt.

Apparently Jim and Pam had stopped at one or more side-

walk cafes on the way home from the movie, where Jim consumed several drinks. (This explains the arrival home at 1am,
quite late for returning from a movie theatre.) At home, Jim
mixed another drink as Pam lined up some white powder on
a table top.

At this point, Diane is a bit vague. Jim had known about
Pam's heroin use, but most agree that apparently he didn't
know how frequently she used it. Diane told me that Pam
seemed able to use it on a daily basis for a while, then merely
stop, suffering rarely from withdrawal. And, Diane said, to
her knowledge, Pam never used heroin with Jim or in his presence, at least until now. Jim disapproved of heroin. This was
confirmed by everyone I talked to. Danny Sugerman, the 14-
year-old high school student who hung out at the Doors'
office and ten years later helped me get *No One Here Gets Out
Alive* published, said Jim actually lectured him about 'the evils
and horrors of heroin'.

So, Diane told me, when Jim saw Pam bent over a line of
white powder, it is possible he thought it was cocaine. Jim
liked cocaine. There is no reason to think he would have done
anything but smile and join Pam on the couch and inhale the
next line of powder.

On the other hand, he could also have sensed, or realized,
that it was heroin. Diane told me that, according to Pam, the
talk about Jim's depression was real. The past year or so,
many projects had been started or discussed – a screenplay
with Michael McClure, a poetry album with John Haeny, a
stage show with Fred Myrow, a book about the Miami trial, an
opera, on and on. None had been completed. Most were still-
born. In addition, Jim was overweight, alcoholic, and impo-
tent (a side-effect of his alcoholism).

The constant drinking only aggravated the depression. Jim
had written a few lines in one of his notebooks that said,
'Leave the informed sense in our wake/you be the Christ on
this package tour/Money beats soul/Last words, last words,

*Overleaf: Left The French doctor's report giving
heart attack as cause of death. Right: The US
Embassy death report.*

RAPPORT MÉDICO-LÉGAL

Je soussigné Max VASSILLE ,médecin assermenté

Docteur en Médecine de la Faculté de PARIS

demeurant à Paris 3I rue du Renard

requis par Monsieur BERRY Robert Commissaire de Police

de l'ARSENAL

Officier de Police Judiciaire,

agissant sur délégation de Monsieur le Procureur de la République

conformément à l'article 74 du Code de Procédure Pénale, serment préa-

lablement prêté de donner mon avis en mon honneur et conscience,

me suis presenté le 3 Juillet I97I à I8 h

à (1) I7 rue Beautreillis escalier A 3e étage droite

afin d'examiner le corps identifié par l'enquête judiciaire comme étant

celui d'un nommé MORRISSON James

âgé de 28 ans.

J'ai constaté : que le corps ne présente en dehors de
lividités cadavériques habituelles aucune trace su
pecte de traumatisme ou de lésion quelconque.Un, p
de sang au niveau des narines.L'evolution d'un éta
de santé de Mr MORRISON telle qu'elle nous a été
raconté par un ami présent sur les lieux peut se
reconstituer ainsi,Mr MORRISON se plaignait depuis
quelques semaines de douleurs précordiales avec
dyspnée d'effort il s'agit manifestement de troubl
coronariens peut être aggravés par l'abus de boiss
alcoolisées.On peut concevoir qu'à l'occasion d'un
changement de température extérieure suivie d'un b
ces troubles se soient aggravés brusquement donnan
le classique infarctus du myocarde cause de mort
subite.De son examen je conclus.
            que la mort a été provoquée par un arrêt
cardiaque (mort naturelle).

Paris, le 3 Juillet I97I

(1) Lieu de l'examen

REPORT OF THE DEATH OF AN AMERICAN CITIZEN

FINAL

nworth American Embassy, Paris, France, August 11, 1971
(Place and date)

Name in full __James Douglas MORRISON__   Occupation __Singer__

Native or naturalized __BORN ON December 8, 1943 AT Clearwater,__   Last known address
in the United States __8216 Norton Avenue, Los Angeles, California__   Florida

Date of death __July__   __3__   __5:00 a.m.__   __1971__   Age __27 years__
(Month)   (Day)   (Hour)   (Minute)   (Year)   (As nearly as can be ascertained)

Place of death __17, rue Beautreillis, Paris 4, France__
(Number and street) or (Hospital or hotel)   (City)   (Country)

Cause of death __Heart Failure__
(Include authority for statement)

As certified by Dr. Max Vassille, 31, rue du Renard, Paris, France

Disposition of the remains __Interred in Pere Lachaise Cemetery, 16th Division, Paris,__
France on July 7, 1971.

Local law as to disinterring remains __May be disinterred at any time upon the request of__
nearest relative or legal representative of the estate. See Decree Law of December
31, 1941, Journal Officiel, January 26-27, 1942, Page 378.

Disposition of the effects __In the custody of Pamela Courson, friend.__

Person or official responsible for custody of effects and accounting therefor __Rear Admiral George S.__
Informed by telegram: Morrison, father.

NAME	ADDRESS	RELATIONSHIP	DATE SENT
N/A			

Copy of this report sent to:

NAME	ADDRESS	RELATIONSHIP	DATE SENT
Rear Admiral George S. Morrison	Chief Naval Operations	Father	August 11, 1971
	OPO 3B - Room 4E 552		
	Pentagon, Washington, D.C. 20350		

Traveling or residing abroad with relatives or friends as follows:

NAME	ADDRESS	RELATIONSHIP
Miss Pamela Courson	17, rue Beautreillis	Friend
	75 - Paris 4, France	

Other known relatives (not given above):

NAME	ADDRESS	RELATIONSHIP
Unknown		

This information and data concerning an inventory of the effects, accounts, etc., have been placed
under File 234 in the correspondence of this office.

Remarks: __U.S. passport number J 900083, issued at Los Angeles, California,__
on August 7, 1968 cancelled and returned to father.

Filing date and place of French Death Certificate: July 3, 1971 at the Town Hall
of Paris 4, France.

(Continue on reverse if necessary.)

Mary Ann Meysenburg

[SEAL]
No fee prescribed.

Vice Consul .... of the United States of America.

▷ Over

I certify that this document is a true copy of the record contained in the files of Passport Services, Department of State.

In testimony whereof, I, _____ GEORGE P. SHULTZ _____, Secretary of State, have hereunto
caused the seal of the Department of State to be affixed and my name subscribed by the Authentication Officer
of the said Department, at the city of Washington, in the District of Columbia, this

_____ day of __February__ 19 84   Service No. __8401708__

George P. Shultz
(Secretary of State)

Killeen B. Masse
(Authentication Officer)

This certificate is not valid if it is altered in any way.

out.' Later, two of Jim's biographers would use these lines to support a theory that his death was likely a suicide.

Diane doesn't dismiss that theory, at least not entirely. She told me that when Jim saw the powder lined up so neatly on the table top, he may have known it wasn't cocaine, but heroin, and knew what dangers lay in its use, especially in combination with alcohol. (When two central nervous system depressants, in this case alcohol and heroin, come together synergistically, they create a knockout punch: one plus one equals six!)

Danny Sugerman told me a slightly different version of the same story. I now know that when Danny edited *No One Here Gets Out Alive* in the late 1970s, he knew that Jim had died of an overdose, but he never told me. But later Danny told me that he and Pamela had shared both heroin and sex after Pam left Diane Gardiner's home and returned to Los Angeles. Danny said that when Pam talked about Jim's death to Danny, she also pledged him not to tell 'Hopkins', who then was trying to interview her. Danny was the one who merged the book's two last chapters into one, which gave him an opportunity to tell the truth. But he remained loyal to Pamela rather than tell what he knew, even though Pam was dead.

I re-interviewed Danny about the same time I talked to Diane Gardiner, in 1981. *No One Here Gets Out Alive* was, by then, a huge success and Jim had been dead for more than ten years, so Danny talked more candidly. (Although he has never yet admitted to me that he had withheld the true story of Jim's death while working on the manuscript.) In our recorded conversation, he told me he had asked Pam about Paris and heroin. At first she told him that Jim would never use heroin. At the time of this conversation, Danny said, both he and Pam were stoned on heroin. 'If he were alive today,' she said, 'he'd kill both of us, Danny.'

Danny told me, 'That didn't answer my question. You couldn't confront Pam on this,' he said. 'It was the most painful moment of her life.'

I asked Danny, 'She never said anything about heroin being a part of his death?'

Danny said, 'I seem to remember her saying something. In

*Singer Patti Smith is just one of thousands who
have paid homage to Morrison at his grave.*

a real stupor, when you're nodding out, you don't know who you're talking to, you don't even know if you're talking, and I feel not unqualified to tell this story, but I feel not awfully secure in its reportage, because I was awful high, too. But I do remember a conversation regarding her guilt and her getting really down on herself...something to the effect: she was busted, Jim found it [the heroin].

'What's this!' Jim said. (As Danny recalled the conversation.)

'It's coke!'

Jim dumped a quantity on the table, deftly pushing it into long, thick lines, probably with the edge of a paper matchbook or a credit card. He inhaled the first line.

Pam said, 'Jim, don't do too much. Jim, don't do too much!'

Danny again: '...rather than say, "Jim, it's smack." Because she had been hiding it from him, and she knew damned well he did not do that. And he did not want her to do it. He saw what heroin did to friends like Tim Hardin. [Another singer-songwriter who died of a heroin overdose.] He knew the hazards of it.

'So I remember a guilt feeling, and an implication...that Jim had discovered her stash and Pam said, "Oh, Jim, it's just coke," which he really wasn't into, at that point anyway, and Jim said, "Let's do some." He put it out and snorted it like it was coke.'

Danny insisted that he didn't know the true story, because this was only one of many that Pamela told, and the one she told most consistently was the 'official' version, of a heart attack in the bathtub. It is, however, the story he believes.

It is the story that was told by Alain Ronay and Agnes Varda to *Paris Match* in 1991, twenty years after Jim's death, that makes this story most real.

Pam took Ronay's arm in the Paris apartment as the doctor was examining Jim's body. Pam said she and Jim had been snorting heroin for two days. Pam said they snorted heroin the night before and again that afternoon, after Jim had taken his walk with Ronay and before he went out to dinner alone. When they returned home from the movie and the bistro, the heroin came out again. In this version, Pam did not mention washing dishes, or say Jim watched home movies. Now Pam said Jim started playing the Doors' recordings, including the first album, which contained the song, 'The End'. She said Jim got out of bed and snorted some more heroin, so, she added, Jim actually had consumed more than she did. She said that one of the Doors' records was playing when they nodded off to sleep.

Ronay quoted Varda as asking, 'Who had the heroin? Was it you?'

Pamela said, 'Of course...'

Pam said she woke up to Jim's heavy breathing. This matched the story she told police. She said that when Jim failed to awake when she shook him, she screamed, and began slapping him 'very, very hard'. Finally, he opened his eyes, but he didn't seem to know where he was. She said she helped him to walk to the bathroom and assisted him into the tub.

Agnes asked her who had run the water in the tub. Pam said she couldn't remember.

Pam told Ronay she returned to the bedroom, fell asleep, waking some time later. When she found Jim missing from their bed, she went to the bathroom and saw him in the tub with blood running from his nose. He started vomiting, she said, so she ran to the kitchen, returning with an orange cooking pot. Three times Jim vomited and each time Pam said she cleaned the pot, returning to bed once more when assured by Jim that he was feeling better.

Varda patted Pam's hand and told her that Jim died at least an hour and a half before the firemen arrived; there was nothing she could do.

Pam said, 'Jim looked so calm. He smiled.' She was in shock.

Varda continued to reassure Pam.

Pam suddenly produced a piece of paper that she said was a marriage application she and Jim had taken out in 1967 in Colorado, but never acted on. She asked her friends if they thought the Paris police would accept it as proof that she and Jim were married.

As the day brightened, the fiction grew. Alan Ronay said he didn't want Jim's death and burial to become the circus that

𝕷𝖆𝖘𝖙 𝖂𝖎𝖑𝖑 𝖆𝖓𝖉 𝕿𝖊𝖘𝖙𝖆𝖒𝖊𝖓𝖙

of

JAMES D. MORRISON

573952

I, JAMES D. MORRISON, being of sound and disposing mind, memory and understanding, and after consideration for all persons, the objects of my bounty, and with full knowledge of the nature and extent of my assets, do hereby make, publish and declare this my Last Will and Testament, as follows:

FIRST: I declare that I am a resident of Los Angeles County, California; that I am unmarried and have no children.

SECOND: I direct the payment of all debts and expenses of last illness.

THIRD: I do hereby devise and bequeath each and every thing of value of which I may die possessed, including real property, personal property and mixed properties to PAMELA S. COURSON of Los Angeles County.

BK 1979 PG 0430

In the event the said PAMELA S. COURSON should predecease me, or fail to survive for a period of three months following the date of my death, then and in such event, the devise and bequest to her shall fail and the same is devised and bequeathed instead to my brother, ANDREW MORRISON of Monterey, California, and to my sister, ANNE R. MORRISON of Coronado Beach, California, to share and share alike; provided, however, further that in the event either of them should predecease me, then and in such event, the devise and bequest shall go to the other.

FOURTH: I do hereby appoint PAMELA S. COURSON and MAX FINK, jointly, Executors, or Executor and Executrix, as the case may be, of my estate, giving to said persons, and each of them, full power of appointment of substitution in their place and stead by their Last Will and Testament, or otherwise.

In the event said PAMELA S. COURSON shall survive me and be living at the time of her appointment, then in such event, bond is hereby waived.

I subscribe my name to this Will this 12 day of February, 1969, at Beverly Hills, California.

ADMITTED TO PROBATE

AUG 17 1971

Attest: William G. Clark, County Clerk
by ___ Deputy

JAMES D. MORRISON

had attended the recent deaths of Jimi Hendrix and Janis Joplin. As Pam and Ronay and Varda – and soon, Robin Wertle – devised a plan for handling Jim's burial, the 'official' version of the death took its final form.

Part of the cover-up was to avoid mentioning anything if anyone telephoned. The first call – forgetting the one from the Count – was from a male friend of the woman from whom Jim and Pam leased the flat. He had seen Pam a few times before Jim joined her in Paris and he wondered if she was free that night to go out with him. She said no, she was going to stay with Jim. The next time the phone rang, Ronay took it. It was Hervé Muller, who hadn't seen Jim in three weeks and was calling to say hello, maybe make some plans. Ronay told Muller that Jim and Pam were away for the weekend.

By now, the news of Jim's death was travelling along the Paris underground and that night (Saturday) about midnight it reached the ears of Cameron Watson, an American expatriate who was then working as a disc jockey in a discotheque called Le Bulle. Two drug-dealers entered Watson's glass-enclosed booth.

'Hey,' said one, 'I just scored three-thousand francs of "H" for Marianne Faithfull and she was crying. She said Jim Morrison is dead.'

Watson knew that Marianne was an addict and that she had been in Paris that week. He did not know that Pam's friend the Count was with Faithfull when the Count called Pam, but Watson believed what Faithfull told him. He stopped the music and said, 'Jim Morrison was found dead this morning.' He made the announcement first in English, then in French.

Jean-Bernard Hebey, who had a radio show on Radio Luxembourg, was at Le Bulle and he took the story to work with him, announcing the death on his show on Sunday. The story now had a large audience and by Monday morning the national newspapers in England were calling the London office of Elektra Records for confirmation.

Clive Selwood, who ran the office, called Elektra's Paris office. The Paris office didn't even know Jim was living in the French capital. Clive then called the American Embassy and the Paris police. Both agencies had no knowledge of the death.

Clive decided to call Bill Siddons in Los Angeles. With the nine-hour time difference, he woke the manager. 'Bill,' he said, 'I can't substantiate it in any way, but we're getting reports that Jim is dead.'

Siddons almost laughed. 'Oh, come on, Clive...' For years, Siddons had heard similar rumours. Jim had died of an overdose or an automobile accident or a fall from a hotel balcony. Clive said he had taken calls from several journalists whom he respected, so Siddons dialled Jim and Pam's Paris number. But there was no answer and he returned to his bed. Awaking several hours later, Siddons tried again and Pam answered. Initially, she denied that Jim was dead, but finally admitted the truth. Pam didn't like the Doors' manager any more than she liked the other Doors, but she knew that he'd take care of business and be able to bring some needed cash. Billy caught the earliest flight to assist with final arrangements and to help Pam pack for a return to California.

At about the same time, Jim's lawyer Max Fink said he received a collect call from Pam. He described her condition as incoherent, greatly agitated. Fink told her to hire a Los Angeles-based private detective named John O'Grady (who had known Jim slightly) and to fly him to Paris immediately to handle everything discreetly. Fink says Pam hung up abruptly, calling back later to explain – calmly now – that everything was under control.

Through the entire weekend, Jim's body had remained on the double bed in the master bedroom, packed in ice, according to Pam's wishes. On Monday, with Ronay's assistance, a mortuary was contracted and a varnished oak coffin was delivered to the apartment. The body was placed inside.

Siddons arrived Tuesday morning and agreed with Pam that the death should be kept quiet. That day and the next, Tuesday and Wednesday, Siddons helped make final arrangements and assisted Pam pack her and Jim's belongings, while Ronay went to Père-Lachaise Cemetery and purchased a plot. This was one of Paris's most famous cemeteries and, according to Pam, Jim had visited it and expressed a desire to be buried there, so he could share a final resting place with Chopin, Bizet, Edith Piaf, Oscar Wilde, Balzac, and Molière.

Ronay handled the purchase of the plot, turning down a location close to Oscar Wilde's tomb, taking a less propitious spot. Siddons and Wertle then visited the funeral home to make final arrangements, requesting a hearse and four pallbearers.

(Danny Sugerman told me that while helping Pam pack, Siddons found heroin in the apartment, but Danny also quoted Pam as saying that regarding Jim's death, Siddons knew only what he was told. In all my conversations with Siddons, he confirmed this. Apparently, he was told nothing about the role heroin played in Jim's death.)

On Wednesday morning, the day before the burial, Pamela filed the death certificate with the American Embassy, identifying Jim only as 'James Douglas Morrison, poet.' Nothing was said about his true celebrity.

The next day, Thursday, Jim's body was lowered into a grave on a tiny plot between two large marble sepulchres at Père-Lachaise. There were only five mourners present: Pam, Bill Siddons, Alain Ronay, Agnes Varda, and Robin Wertle.

In the years that followed, Pam fought for acceptance as Jim's heir and wife. Initially, it seemed quite simple. Jim had had his lawyer, Max Fink, draft a simple, two-page will in 1969, naming Pamela S. Courson as his sole heir and, with Fink, his co-executor. (In the event that Pam died first, Jim's estate was to be shared equally by his brother and sister.)

In November 1971, four months after Jim died, in an effort to bolster her claim, and to be granted an allowance and an advance from the estate – which was then still in probate – Pam filed a 'declaration in support of widow's allowance', claiming 'at all times since September 30, 1967, I have considered that I was married to James D. Morrison, and that I was in fact his wife at the time of his death and am now his widow'. It was in 1967, as 'Light My Fire' was finally dropping off the charts, that Pam said she and Jim spent a night in Colorado Springs. Earlier, she had Jim ask Max Fink which states had the loosest laws recognizing common law marriage.

In her court statement, Pam said, 'Jim reported to me that he learned from an attorney that to create a marriage in the state of Colorado it was sufficient if two people stayed together, had marital relations and agreed to thereby be husband and wife, if in fact they thereafter conducted and held themselves out as each other's spouse. We spent the night at a hotel, had sexual relations and agreed that we would forever after be husband and wife. We very briefly honeymooned in Colorado and then continued our [the Doors] tour.'

Pam's statement went on to say that during their relationship, all her living expenses were paid from Jim's earnings. All credit card charges were paid, she said, her medical, dental, clothing, and entertainment expenses were paid, and she and Jim were given $2,500 in cash each month for incidentals. Now, she said, she was penniless.

In December 1971, the three surviving Doors filed papers of their own in court, making claims against the Morrison estate, most of it for a loan they said Jim had taken to help pay some of his legal costs. Although the sum asked, less than $36,000, was small, considering the size of the estate, it was sufficient to bottle things up in court for two years. Then in April 1974, the Doors came back with another lawsuit, now requesting repayment of a $250,000 loan allegedly made by the Doors Corporation to Jim as an advance against his share of future royalties. At the same time, Max Fink, who continued to represent the other Doors, submitted a bill for approximately $75,000 for work done on the Phoenix and Miami trials. Next the Miami law firm filed suit for unpaid services.

Eventually, a compromise was reached. Pam relented, agreeing to pay everyone. Max Fink said he authorized a loan to Pam in the interim, much of which was spent on a mink coat and a yellow Volkswagen Beetle. Then, as the final accounting of the estate was being made, Pam died. If she had lived, she would have received about $500,000 right away, plus a quarter of everything the Doors would make in the future, a sum that subsequently proved to be worth millions.

What really happened in Paris on July 3, 1971?

I am certain that Jim died of an overdose of heroin, complicated by the alcohol level in his bloodstream. What generally happens when these two 'drugs' come together and deliver their synergistic hammer-blow, is described as a 'massive pul-

Morrison's grave in Père-Lachaise cemetery,
Paris, surrounded by gifts and plaques from fans.

monary edema', a kind of mega heart attack, where the victim, poisoned by the combination, slumps, froth spilling from his mouth and nostrils.

Of course, no one will ever know. The only person present at the time of Jim's death was Pamela, who may not even have known herself what happened, and if she did, she took the full story to her grave. Obviously, she had something to do with Jim's death, may even have unwittingly caused it, at least in her own mind, by having the heroin in the apartment and sharing it with him.

I thought it was interesting that before signing over the rights to their daughter's life to Oliver Stone for his movie *The Doors*, her parents had it written into the contract that the script make no connection whatsoever between Pamela and Jim's death. In other words, if Stone was going to portray Jim's death in any way, he was to stick to the 'official' version. (Which he did.) Did Pam's parents know what happened, and share their daughter's grief and guilt? Had they become partners in the conspiracy to cover up the true cause of Jim's death?

When I was researching *No One Here Gets Out Alive*, I met Pam once, over lunch. I left the restaurant feeling I had just spent a couple of hours with the most beautiful, fragile, vulnerable, and manipulative woman I had ever met, but I had learned very little about Jim, or her, or their relationship. And I was told nothing about Jim's death.

I asked her why she had agreed to meet me. She said Jim had liked me, and I had written positive stories about him and the Doors. She also wanted to know why I was writing the book. I told her that I was more affected by Jim's death than I thought our relationship warranted and I wanted to find out why. She said nothing, merely nodded.

At the time of the meeting, two years after Jim's death, I had no idea what Pam was doing for a living. She avoided answering such questions by saying only that she was trying to keep Jim's memory alive and untarnished. For example, she told me she had won a fight to keep 'Light My Fire' from being sold for a television commercial. All her other comments were superficial and unrevealing. She seemed nervous, but in control of the situation, as if she were caught in a scene she wanted to end, and was handling it, nonetheless.

Years later, Danny Sugerman, and others, told me her life was a mess. Danny said he had spent a lot of time with her, frequently shared his own heroin with her, sometimes gave her part of the $75 a week that he was getting from Ray Manzarek (as Manzarek's publicist). Danny said he thought Pam was seriously disturbed, said she sometimes sat near the telephone, waiting for Jim to call. Danny quoted her as saying, 'My old man hasn't called! He promised me he'd call!'

Implying that Jim was alive, all evidence – and her own tortured stories – to the contrary.

When Pam died, on 25 April 1974, at age 27 – Jim's age when he died – she was working as a prostitute, something she often said that Jim had predicted was her destiny. A man who had worked as Jim's occasional limousine driver was her live-in boyfriend and it was clear, from the autopsy, that an overdose of heroin was the cause of death.

Pam once had asked Max Fink to draw up her will, but he refused, so she died intestate, which meant her quarter-share of all future Doors earnings went to her next-of-kin, her parents, Columbus (Corky) Courson, and his wife Pearl (Penny). Almost immediately, Jim's parents, Admiral George Morrison and his wife Clara, entered the fray, demanding their 'fair share' as stated in the California probate code. On 10 January 1975, the two sets of parents signed an agreement dividing equally the proceeds from Jim's quarter-share of all Doors revenue, but it was 1979 before all the loose ends were tied up and the parents started receiving any money.

Since then, Jim's share of the Doors' earnings have been worth several hundreds of thousands of dollars, at the peak more than a million dollars a year. Today, the Coursons have homes in Santa Barbara and Palm Springs and the Morrisons own substantial property in Orange and San Diego Counties. I think Jim would be amused that his posthumous fortune is being shared by a retired high school principal and a retired Navy admiral, authority figures for whom he had no time or respect when he was alive.

You can't get away with irony like that in fiction.

VII

WEIRD SCENES INSIDE THE
GOLD MINE

BY 1973, there was someone in San Francisco who claimed to be (1) Jim Morrison, (2) Jim Morrison's reincarnation, or (3) someone who could put you in touch with Jim Morrison. The living room of his apartment had been turned into a shrine, with posters and fresh flowers brought in every day. Not long afterward, he was arrested for writing cheques in Jim's name.

In Los Angeles, one of the FM stations began playing a 'mystery tape' that sounded a near-perfect copy of Jim's voice and someone – it's not sure who – paid a visit to a journalist who had known Jim, so upsetting the journalist that he still won't say it was or wasn't the man he once interviewed.

Old girlfriends marched on New York publishers with poetry they claimed Jim had helped them write, as other publishers rejected memoirs and screenplays and novels by the score, all inspired by the Lizard King. And Elektra Records released another album, another repackaging of old hits, this one in quadrophonic sound.

In 1974, the mysterious, sound-alike tape was released by Capitol Records as a 45 rpm single by an artist identified only as 'Phantom'. An FBI voiceprint check in New York, requested by one of the radio stations, proved negative.

That's the way it's gone for 20 years. For a while, the grave was unmarked except by the fans, graffiti and trash, and when the Doors paid to have a marker made, it was promptly stolen.

On and on.

The *maitre d'* at the Ivy assured me that there was no reservation for anyone named Stone, and the impression I got was that the restaurant had more bookings per chair than a flight to Hawaii on United. I was early. I said I'd hang around for Oliver.

'Oliver?' the *maitre d'* asked. 'Oliver Stone, the director?' I nodded. 'Ah, well, then, of course, if Mr Stone comes, we can find a table, of course.'

Down the hall I saw Jim Morrison using the pay phone. I'd forgotten he was so tall. I laughed at myself. Morrison had been dead for nearly 20 years and this was Val Kilmer, the actor selected by Stone to play the sixties Lizard King. It was eerie. The start of principal photography was two months off, and Kilmer was already into the part: the leather wardrobe, the shaggy hair, the courtly manner, the boyish grin.

After Kilmer hung up the phone, I introduced myself and told him the *maitre d'* claimed there was no reservation. 'Not to worry,' said Kilmer, reaching for the phone again. He dialled Stone's office and said, 'Jerry and I are at the Ivy, and they say there's no reservation for Oliver. You better have somebody call down here and say Oliver Stone in a real loud voice right away.' No sooner had the phone been returned to the cradle than the *maitre d'* appeared and said, 'I can take you to your table now.'

At last. The Jim Morrison movie was really getting made. I had good reason to think it never would. I sold the movie rights to *No One Here Gets Out Alive* four times in seven years. That's probably no record, but in some circles in the 1980s, the Morrison story came to be regarded as one of those films that couldn't, or shouldn't, be made. Now that the project was finally under way – with Oliver Stone the writer-director – I looked back at the labyrinthine trail with some amazement. Over the years, dozens had been involved: Allan Carr, William Friedkin, Jerry Weintraub, Brian De Palma, Aaron Russo, Golan and Globus, Paul Schrader, Francis Coppola, Charlie Sheen, Irving Azoff, and Martin Scorsese among the directors and producers, and to play Morrison, John Travolta, Jason Patric, Keanu Reeves, Michael O'Keefe, Gregory Harrison, Michael Ontkean, Steven Bauer, Christopher Lambert, the lead singers from INXS (Michael Hutchence) and

U2 (Bono), Timothy Bottoms, Richard Gere, and Tom Cruise. The story of the Doors movie is one of pissing contests and soaring egos, of complicated fuck-you option deals and people changing partners and sides, of Indians dancing on a Malibu beach and hundreds dancing on Morrison's grave. It is the story of parents and siblings, along with the surviving Doors and who knows how many agents and lawyers and other movie-biz types, all sides talking about karma and curses and the forces of evil and light, bickering over the Morrison myth and who has the right to do what with it.

Much of the early Morrison movie talk concerned making a documentary. In July 1981, on the tenth anniversary of Jim's death, a Boston film maker accompanied the surviving Doors to Paris, where they encountered a cluster of mournful fans gathered at Jim's grave. Witnesses say the band's keyboardist, Ray Manzarek, seized the moment as the cameras began to roll and climbed onto a nearby tombstone to make a fervent speech: 'Do you think Jim Morrison is here? I never saw the body! Jim's too big for this little grave, man! Do you really think he's dead?'

The Bostonian's documentary was not completed and a second try by a Hollywood film maker almost failed as well, until the Doors stepped in and assumed financial control. *A Tribute to Jim Morrison* runs an hour in length and blends new interviews with footage from concerts and the Doors' own early documentary, *Feast of Friends*.

Jim had been dead for nine years when my biography was published and when it topped *The New York Times* best-seller list and remained on that list for nine months, it was no surprise that Hollywood showed some interest. Rock and roll had been a key ingredient in several recent films, including *Saturday Night Fever* (1977), *Grease* and *The Buddy Holly Story* (both 1978), *The Rose* (1979) and the *Blues Brothers* (1980), all selling millions of albums as well as tickets.

In 1981, Sasha Harari, a recent immigrant from Israel, offered $50,000 for the film rights to my book. Harari then got *Grease* producer Allan Carr to write the cheque, with a second payment of $275,000 promised if the film went into production.

About the same time, the star of *Grease* and *Saturday Night Fever*, John Travolta, told Ray Manzarek that he wanted the film's lead role. Manzarek took Travolta on a crawl of Jim's favourite bars and actually talked about reuniting the Doors, with Travolta taking Morrison's place as vocalist. 'There was nothing around at the time that seemed as exciting to me,' Travolta said. 'The music was resurging, and I was really hot to do it.' The actor began rehearsing to Jim's videotapes, and he was good.

In 1981, with Allan Carr's $275,000 offer fresh in my fantasy, I was flown to California and put up in the choicest new hotel in Beverly Hills, L'Hermitage. A long, white limousine took me to Warner Bros., where the director of *The Exorcist* and *The French Connection*, William Friedkin, said he wanted me to write the script with Ray Manzarek. But the deal fell apart, and in Spring 1982, Allan Carr said I had dragged him into a fraudulent contract and demanded that I return the $50,000.

Three months later, *Rolling Stone* put Jim on the cover, the headline read, 'He's hot, he's sexy, and he's dead,' and the issue became one of the magazine's all-time best-sellers. Soon after that, Allan Carr offered a new contract and made another token payment, but it was a lost cause. The Doors had decided Carr didn't understand Jim, and as for Travolta, he was a nice guy, but Jim wasn't nice. Said drummer John Densmore, 'Jim was scary.'

Working with Travolta, director Brian De Palma began writing a script titled *Fire*, about a rock star who faked his death. Largely because *Eddie and the Cruisers*, a film that took a similar plot line, was in development, De Palma couldn't get a studio interested. Meanwhile, others approached Sasha Harari and the Doors, including Francis Coppola and Martin Scorsese, while Jim's sister Anne and her husband announced they were making a documentary *and* a feature film.

In 1985, Harari convinced the three Doors to renew their support, and the man who had promoted Doors concerts in San Francisco and New York in the 1960s, Bill Graham, was brought in to assist in negotiations with the Coursons and the Morrisons. By the time those talks were complete, the Coursons were promised that the movie would not be based on my book, which Mr Courson called a 'vile despicable rip-off', and that their daughter would not be shown having anything to do with the singer's death. In the agreement with the Morrisons, a clause specified that no mention of them would be made in the film; this was later altered to allow one, innocuous scene.

Harari called Oliver Stone's agent to ask if he'd be interested in directing the film. Harari was told he missed Stone by a day. Stone had just gone to the Philippines to make *Platoon*.

From 1985 to 1987, the project languished at Columbia Pictures, who subsequently dropped it when the studio got a new chairman. That was the year that *La Bamba* proved once again that a rock and roll story could work in film. More important, 1987 marked the twentieth anniversary of the 'Summer of Love', a media event that suggested a new psychedelic era might be standing in the wings – or, at the least, was worth a nostalgic look. United Artists and Warner Brothers showed interest in the Doors' story, but it went to Imagine Films, a company started by the actor Ron Howard following his success directing *Coccoon*. The efforts of the first screenwriter were rejected, however, and a second writer was given the assignment. That was when the Writers Guild went on strike in 1988.

In Hollywood there is something called *force majeure*, French for an 'Act of God'. As it is applied in Hollywood business practice, it can mean that if there is a writers' or directors' or actors' strike, all contracts in force at the time of the strike's beginning are extended for the length of the strike. When the writers' strike lasted six months, Imagine assumed its option on the Doors' life story and rights to the Doors' music were extended for a like period.

No way. It was a legally unsupportable tradition, said the Doors' legal representatives. It wasn't in writing and if Imagine didn't come up with $750,000 by 1 August 1988, when the option expired, all rights would revert to the Doors. Now, that may not seem a large figure by Hollywood standards, but Imagine had taken a terrible beating in the stock market crash the previous year and, according to some, the production company's cupboard was bare.

Producers and agents began circling. I started getting calls from Charlie Sheen, who said he wanted the movie rights and intended to produce the film and co-write a script on specula- tion with a friend, Scott Goldman. He said he had a produc- tion deal with Orion and U2's lead singer, Bono, was ready to play Morrison. At that time, Bono included a Doors medley in his band's performances.

'I've seen U2 in concert four times,' Sheen told me, 'and Bono does Morrison so fucking great, it's chilling. This is how it'll happen. We write the script in three weeks. Normally, I take ten days, but this is special. We send the script to you first, you tell me what you want. Sound good to you?' He told me to have my agent call his friend Goldman.

My agent did that and then called me and said, 'Goldman is 23, and everything I say, he says, "Oh, wow, that's really radi- cal, what do we do now?" ' I never heard from Sheen again.

The August deadline loomed and, at the final moment, who should come riding to Imagine's rescue but Carolco, the com- pany that made its early fortune with the Rambo films. The Doors were paid $750,000, thus keeping the rights to the band's likenesses, story, and songs from reverting to the three surviving band members, the Coursons and the Morrisons. Once again, Jim belonged to Hollywood.

Still another screenwriter was hired, but his script was rejected, too. Oliver Stone claims he first became involved in discussions of a Doors movie as early as 1986 and now with his own two-picture deal in place at Carolco, Stone became firmly attached to the project. Stone devoured Jim's poetry and my book. He watched the Doors' video and film collec- tion over and over again. He visited the scenes of the singer's life. He listened to the music constantly. Then he wrote a screenplay, in collaboration with J. Randal Johnson.

Soon after that, Oliver flew me to Los Angeles, where at the Ivy I met Val Kilmer. As we ordered the first glasses of wine, waiting for Stone to join us, I couldn't get over how much Kilmer looked like Morrison. From watching him as the rene- gade swordsman in *Willow*, I knew he had the right colouring, cheekbones, and muscled jaw. Now he was in character. Cowboy boots, hair the right length. He even blinked in precisely the same sleepy way that Morrison blinked and tilted his head shyly.

'I feel very lucky,' Kilmer said. 'Everybody wanted the part. Timothy Bottoms, Tom Cruise. Actors do the best they've ever done when they work with Oliver.'

We ordered more wine – of course we did, wasn't I drinking with Morrison again?—and I asked Kilmer how old he was. He told me he was 30. I said, 'You were just a kid in the sixties.'

He agreed, 'Yeah, I was, but I had an older brother who took me to a Jimi Hendrix concert and I've read a lot.' He asked if I had the original tapes of my interviews with Jim, because he wanted to copy Jim's voice.

If Kilmer bore surface similarities to Morrison, Stone's resemblance to the musician ran even deeper. They were only a couple of years apart in age, and they came from similar Establishment backgrounds. Stone's father was a Wall Street stockbroker, Morrison's a Navy officer. Both were college graduates. There was a common interest in writing and film; they experienced the world within verbal and visual contexts.

More important, I sensed a shared, anarchic intensity. There was a brash daring to experiment, coupled with a fierce determination to find emotional buttons and to push them hard. They liked to give people the finger, to test them. Getting a reaction was important.

Professionally, they looked for an audience's soft spots and attacked with guns and concepts blazing, or with such calculated control it was maddening. Oliver used great, looping, 360-degree pans that increased the pressure on the viewer in the same way that Jim inserted long silences into his songs. Oliver, as a writer, pulled a bloody head from a shoulder bag (*Year of the Dragon*), impaled a prison guard on a wall peg (*Midnight Express*), had the star throw his face into a heap of cocaine (*Scarface*), and, as the director of *Platoon*, had the good guy die with his arms out-thrust like the crucified Christ's. Jim posed for publicity pictures with an erection, frequently threw himself into the concert audience, vomited blood in one of rock's earliest videos, and in that notorious performance in Miami, dropped his pants at least part-way.

In Oliver, I sensed a volcano at rest. After he joined us at the table, I told him, 'When I first heard your name associated with the project, I thought: Stone's not particularly subtle, but neither was Jim. You're perfect for each other.' Stone showed his trademark gap-toothed grin.

Stone said he had a copy of a diary: a groupie's affair with the Shaman/Lizard King. He looked at Val and said, 'Everything is in there! This is a woman who was naked with Morrison many times! She talks about his cock! He's so gentle and loving. And then he turns into a complete shit. A complete Jekyll and Hyde.'

I returned to Los Angeles in May to watch a day's shooting as Stone's guest. The first thing I did was read the script, but Stone said I couldn't take it with me – I had to read it in an office at Carolco. I liked the script, as a script, but I was appalled by the liberties Stone had taken with both character and chronology. When Oliver's name was first attached to the Morrison film project, he was being criticized for the way he fictionalized Ron Kovic's life story in his film adaptation of Kovic's book, *Born on the Fourth of July*. Initially, Oliver denied the charges, but eventually he said he told 'small lies in order to reveal larger truths'. He went on to win the Oscar for Best Director for that film, but his reputation was sullied nonetheless, as he became cinema's answer to gonzo journalism, where you never let the facts get in the way of a good story. It appeared – at least in the script – that Stone was doing it again with what was then called 'The Doors Project'.

While it was true that Morrison was a sexual figure in practice as well as image – despite the impotence that plagued his last couple of years – the amount of sex in the script seemed disproportionate: more women dropped to their knees than you saw during an old-style Catholic Mass. Meg Ryan, who played Pam, absolutely refused to perform one of the scenes. (Even so, she showed her breasts and engaged in several vivid sexual performances.) When asked about Oliver's vision of Morrison, Val Kilmer said, 'It was tits and acid.'

Plus, Morrison's intelligence, gentlemanly manner, and

sense of humour were, to use a phrase Stone should recognize, missing in action.

I had a problem with the way Patricia Kennealy was portrayed. She was the magazine editor who had married Jim in a handfasting ceremony that was said to blend souls on a karmic and cosmic plane that has an effect on future incarnations of the two involved. Patricia happily agreed to play the part of the priestess who performed the handfasting. But when she arrived on the set to marry Val Kilmer to Kathleen Quinlan (who played the Kennealy part), she was given only the pages of her scene. When Stone warned her, 'I have you doing things in the script you didn't do,' she replied, 'That's okay, so long as they aren't things I wouldn't do.' She came to regret that.

After reading the script, I called her and told her that she had become three characters merged into one. For example, Oliver had her involved in a cocaine-induced blood orgy the first time that she and Jim met, when in reality they merely shook hands – while the orgy came late in Jim's life and involved a different woman [Magda].

In another scene, in a shower stall backstage at New Haven, Patricia asked Jim how much his father loved him. He held his fingers an inch apart. Patricia then asked how his mother felt. Jim held his fingers about an inch and a half apart. Patricia wasn't in New Haven, didn't meet Jim until much later, and told me that the entire scene was made up.

More important was Oliver's major theme: Morrison as shaman, the tribe's medicine man or priest. If Jim's tribe was the sixties generation, Oliver figured, surely Jim was the ecclesiastic. Didn't Jim himself say that the soul of a dying Indian leaped into his head at age five? As a college student, didn't he believe he could 'diagnose' an audience and devise a way to 'treat' it through manipulation? Didn't all those psychedelic drugs consumed during the sixties point in the same direction? Or was the shaman just another of Jim's images, like the Erotic Politician and the Lizard King?

When I saw Oliver the next day on the set, I asked him how it was going. He said it was hard. I looked puzzled, I guess, because he went on to explain that 'the shaman thing, it's going to be hard to get that across'.

I said, 'Yeah, you make a pretty big deal of it.'
He said, 'It's my hook. It's my hook.'
I asked Oliver, 'Was this always the way you felt about Jim?' He said yes, it was, even when he was in the jungle in Vietnam.

In the version of the film that reached the screen, the first scene shows the five-year-old Morrison encountering the dying Indian, and from that point forward there is a bald-headed Indian appearing in most of the important scenes, until in the final scene, just before Pam discovers Jim dead in the bathtub, the Indian is shown sneaking out of the bathroom and down the hall. There are flashbacks to the dying Indian, peyote rituals and hallucinations in the California desert, Indian drawings on the wall of a cave, ghost-like Indians dancing with Jim on the concert stage. Sorry, Oliver, but if that's your hook, I'm the fish that got away.

In another scene, Jim freaks out when he hears his band's biggest hit song, 'Light My Fire', used for a car commercial, when in reality, Jim stopped Chrysler or Buick or whoever it was from using the song (after the other Doors signed over the rights without him) and the commercial never happened. I could go on.

And yet, all of these changes were made while painstaking attention was being paid to re-creating the smallest environmental detail. When I told Robby Krieger that Oliver's office had called me repeatedly to determine precisely when certain pictures in my book were taken, to establish accurate wardrobe chronology, he admitted that the wardrobe was flawless. When Patricia Kennealy was flown to Hollywood to perform the handfasting, she found that her New York apartment had been duplicated so perfectly that she saw bills bearing her Lower East Side address on the desk.

And the truth is, most of the film is accurate, most of the events depicted did occur more or less as written and filmed. And it appears that millions of dollars were spent replicating not only the Whisky a Go-Go and the sixties concert halls (with up to 3,000 extras in attendance), but also the Sunset Strip and the Haight-Ashbury section of San Francisco. As someone who was there, let me say that Oliver really took me back, whip-lashing me through my past with stunning accuracy. And if the Ed Sullivan, Andy Warhol, and Truman Capote characters in the film appeared to be made of *papier maché*, Val Kilmer as Jim was bang-on. He looked like Jim, he talked and sang like Jim, and he moved like Jim. The film was, in fact, a one-man tour de force.

Unfortunately, the script did not give Val Kilmer the dimension that Jim deserved, and that history demanded. Oh, Jim was portrayed accurately enough, but only up to a point. Oliver's 'take' on Jim showed him to be a mean, self-indulgent, self-destructive drunk. All true, of course. But he also was charming, witty, intelligent, articulate, and he had a sense of humour about himself. I believe the interviews in this book and, I hope, in a few of the stories I've told, a fuller, more accurate portrait emerges. Oliver's movie gives a narrow, ugly picture. When Jim finally lifted the last bottle to his lips, and drained it, many in the film's audience were quite content to see him go take a bath. As I left the theatre after one viewing, I heard someone say, 'I couldn't wait for that sonofabitch to die.' I went home feeling as if Oliver had betrayed Jim. I don't think Jim should be held up as a role model for younger generations. But when you trash a man as thoroughly as Oliver Stone trashed Jim Morrison in *The Doors*, the good stuff that Jim had to say gets trashed as well.

I remember the sixties – and Jim – as being more fun. I remember that there was more hope. Looking back now, we may seem to have been naive, but there was an innocence and optimism that Oliver missed. Maybe it's because he was in Vietnam at the time, losing his.

Maybe so and maybe not. Sure enough, the Doors had a dark side. And everyone is entitled to his or her 'take' on Jim's life. More than anyone else I've known or met, Jim was like the elephant described by a group of blind men; each blind man, grabbing a different piece of the elephant's anatomy, inevitably described it differently. So if this is what Oliver Stone saw in his mind's eye, if Oliver wants to fictionalize Jim's life, and turn him into an Indian shaman, why not? Because Jim did the same thing. I just think that Oliver made a bigger deal of it than Jim ever did.

I believe that from an early age, at least from adolescence, Jim thought of himself in larger-than-life proportions. Most people in high school struggle to find their identity. Jim wanted something more; he wanted to create it. As a student at Clearwater Junior College, at Florida State University, and at UCLA, he continued his self-creation. As a rock star in the sixties, his fantasies were introduced to an audience that wanted to believe anything and everything. Revolt and getting back at your parents. Death. Sex. Drugs. Rock and roll. Themes for an eternity.

Following one of the entertainment business's Golden Rules, Jim gave them what they wanted.

And what of his enduring popularity?

Jim followed another Golden Rule: he left his audience wanting more.

THE
INTERVIEWS

LOS ANGELES
FREE PRESS
John Carpenter
Summer 1968

John Carpenter was the music editor of the *Los Angeles
Free Press*, a weekly 'underground' newspaper
distributed throughout Southern California. Like Jim,
he was a big drinker, and the interview stretched
over all of one day, starting with a breakfast laced with
Bloody Marys and ending in the Phone Booth, Jim's
favourite topless bar.

As detailed earlier, in the biographical section of this
book, John took the transcript of the tape to Jim for
approval. Jim added some clarification and Pamela took
a blue pencil to the interview, slashing uncounted
hundreds of paragraphs where she felt Jim was making
an ass of himself. The interview survived her editing,
revealing Jim's robust delight in life.

JOHN CARPENTER: *How did the cover on* Strange Days *come about?*
JIM MORRISON: I hated that cover on the first album. So I said, 'I don't want to be on this cover. Where is that? Put a chick on it or something. Let's have a dandelion or a design.' The title, *Strange Days* came and everybody said yeah, 'cause that was where we were, what was happening. It was so right.

Originally I wanted us in a room surrounded by about 30 dogs, but that was impossible 'cause we couldn't get the dogs and everybody was saying, 'What do you want dogs for?' And I said that it was symbolic that it spelled God backwards. *[Laughs]* Finally we ended up leaving it up to the art director and the photographer. We wanted some real freaks though, and he came out with a typical side show thing. It looked European. It was better than having our fucking faces on it though.

What place do albums have as art forms to you?
I believe they've replaced books. Really. Books and movies. They're better than movies 'cause a movie you see maybe once or twice, then later on television maybe. But a fucking album man, it's more influential than any art form going. Everybody digs them. They've got about 40 of them in their houses and some of them you listen to 50 times, like the Stones' albums or Dylan's.

You don't listen to the Beatles much anymore, but there are certain albums that just go on and on. You measure your progress mentally by your records, like when you were really young what you had then, Harry Belafonte, you know, Calypso, Fats Domino, Elvis Presley.

You guys are only working weekends now, aren't you?
No, not really. I think we work a lot. More than most people think. Like after the [Hollywood] Bowl we go to Texas, then to Vancouver, Seattle, then jump to the East Coast, Montreal and blah, blah, blah. Take three weeks off in August for the film, then we go to Europe. Man, we work an awful lot!

Do you still read a lot?
No, not as much as I used to. I'm not as prolific a writer either. Like when, a while ago, I was living in this abandoned office building, sleeping on the roof, you know the tale. *[Laughs]* And all of a sudden, I threw away all my notebooks that I'd been keeping since high school and these songs just kept coming

to me. Something about the moon, I don't remember.

Well, I'd have to make up words as fast as I could in order to hold onto the melody – you know a lot of people don't know it, but I write a lot of the melodies too – later, all that would be left would be the words 'cause I couldn't hold on to them. The words were left in a sort of vague idea. In those days when I heard a song, I heard it as an entire performance. Taking place, you know, with the audience, the band and the singer. Everything. It was kind of like a prediction of the future. It was all there.

How did the ending to 'The End' come about? Is the Whisky a Go-Go story true?

I used to have this magic formula, like, to break into the subconscious. I would lay there and say over and over 'Fuck the mother, kill the father. Fuck the mother, kill the father.' You can really get into your head just repeating that slogan over and over. Just saying it can be the thing . . .

That mantra can never become meaningless. It's too basic and can never become just words 'cause as long as you're saying it, you can never be unconscious. That all came from up here.

That really shook the Whisky audience up when you did it. Have you ever really gotten through to an audience like the first time you went over and got mobbed and all?

Not like the thing that's in my mind. I think the day that thing happens it will be all over. The End. Where would you go from there? If everyone, even for a split second, became one. They could never come back. No, I don't think it can ever happen, not like it is in my head.

My audiences . . .they usually get pretty turned on. It's like saying at first you're the audience and we're up here, you're down there. Then all of a sudden there you are and you're right there just like us . . . it's out of sight. When they know 'You're just like us,' it breaks down all the barriers and I like that a lot.

I've heard a lot of talk from friends in England, and some of the groups from there, that a lot of hostility will be aimed your way when you go over there. You know, as America's super-sex group and all.

Yeah? . . . hmmm, there's gonna be a bit of hostility, huh? That's a good prediction, yeah, a prediction of the future. There is going to be a little bit of hostility and if there isn't, I'm going to be a little bit disappointed. The more hostility, the better. *[Laughs]* Opposition is true friendship, ha!

[Knock on the door. It's the maid.]

Come on in, we're splitting anyway.

MAID: *I'm ready if you are, [Waits] I'm ready if you are . . . I know you like a clean bed. [Leaves room to get cleaning materials.]*

I knew this was going to be good, but not that good. Let's split right after we hear what else she has to say. *[Laughs]*

MAID: *I'm ready for you if you're ready for me.*

Come here for a little peace and quiet and everyone keeps pushing me.

MAID: *Is that right? [Laughs] Yeah, just keeps on doin' it. Well, I'm ready for you if you're ready for me. [Hums]*

Please, no singing, this is a holiday. I'm on holiday.

[In the elevator.]

Where were you living a year ago?

A year ago? At the Tropicana. Yeah, I started that whole scene. Put it on the map. We used to have lots of fun there. Yeah, it's boisterous. Them [the band] was there, nice guys.

[In the street on the way to the Doors' office. Sunset to Santa Monica on foot.]

Man, I really feel good.

You had your album all ready to go and you went back into the studio to add some things, then I hear you left if alone.

Yeah, we didn't do it. I was going to add some poetry where the little space is between the cuts. But who wants to listen to some cat talking. The music is what's happening. That's what they want to hear. Anybody can talk, but how many cats can play music and sing?

It seems strange to walk in L.A.

Yeah, doesn't it man! *[Bike rider yells, honks, U-turns]* Who was that? It's Babe *[the Doors' road manager]*.

BABE: *Where you headed, the office? [Babe goes on ahead on his bike.]*

He's a happy cat, you know? He's either a genius or really dumb, I haven't found out which. He sure knows how to have a good time. A happy cat.

Oh, there was this chick once, you know, at a concert. She came back stage and said that there was this person that wanted to meet me. She said it was her friend and she was deaf and dumb so I went through this number, you know, drawing pictures, sign language, and it turns out she was putting me on. *[Laughs]*

I really dig L.A. IN THE SUMMER. Winters are a drag, but Summer's pretty nice.

I really dig L.A. Really a lot.

[Topless bar. Babe joins us, drinks are there.]

[To Babe] Dig you, big drinker.

BABE: *[Indicating a dancer.] Can you imagine the babies that chick could have?*
That's bad for their tits when they dance topless. Ask any topless dancer. If they lose them it would be like losing your head . . . She doesn't work too hard. Just sort of stands there . . . Bless this house and all that are in it.
[Later]
[Pointing to new dancer] She's too satirical. She doesn't take anything seriously. I get the feeling that if you spent a lot of time in a place like this you'd corrupt your soul. Corrode it completely. But let's hold off that. Can you imagine bringing your secretary in here? Ha!
['If I Were a Carpenter' by the Four Tops on juke]
If I were a carpenter and you were a lady, would you marry me anyway?
BABE: *No. No. If you were a good natured prostitute I might, maybe. Everybody knows that prostitutes make the best wives, Henry Miller taught us that, right, John?*
Henry who? [To Morrison] What do you think about what's been printed about you and the stuff you hear back all the time? Did you read the Post *magazine thing?*
Yeah, I read it. You know, I knew she was going to do it that way. Journalists are people, you know, and the chicks . . . she did a number, man. Yeah, if you don't really come on to them, they feel neglected, you know? She ended up doing a number. It was written good though. You really felt like you were there. It lies a lot of times. I hear things back all the time that I'm supposed to have done.
Hey, Babe, you're gonna be a famous person one of these days and you should learn to hold your tongue. Especially in front of the press. How'd you like to wake up one day and you've said something off the top of your head and have to read about it the next day, like that is supposed to be where you're at.
The mentality of the writer is like the 'psychology' of the voyeur. Journalists never seem to speak about themselves like other people do. They absorb like a sponge and never really discuss their own psyche. I think that . . . like . . . I think art, which is like beauty, is the revelation of beauty, beauty is an absolute, you dig? And I think it's rooted in a disinterested perception of the real world. Striking an evenness, a balance between object and receiver, like revealing the world with no connotation at all. None, no bullshit.
You know when you've done it, and if you haven't, you are still

on the way. But me, if I get something really good, I'm gonna lay it out, do you dig? But a lot of it gets into that 'He was standing there on the street step with his eyeball exposed.' My perspective when people ask me questions is like I tell them where it's at over and over and over again. Me, me, me . . . But then that's only part of it, part of the thing; not the whole answer.

There's a little more to it than that. Yeah, like I think that there is a sub-world in which everybody is sleeping. This whole other world that everybody's trying to forget, but which we remember, immediately everybody knows it. But people love the game. The Game. They really dig it and nobody is supposed to admit that it's a game. They won't. If they did, then they would ruin the game.

In the middle of the baseball game, like if someone ran out and said, 'It's a game, man, just a fucking game, this is fucked. Are you kidding me? It's just a fucking game.' Well, everybody would say, 'Wow, man, get that fucking clown out of here.' They'd go home, eat a big meal, ball their old lady, and then be right there. He who laughs last, laughs his ass off.

BABE: *Can you dig that? Do you know what he's saying? I think you're serious. I haven't been able to dig it completely yet, but it's there. I know it's there.*

[Later]

It's weird. People in here, after the initial glimpse, just start going on their own trips, talking, eating, drinking. Do you know what it is? I bet that was the appeal of the brothel. Like the atmosphere, a place for conversation.

Man, this is the place I'd really like to work, only instead of business men, it would be business women, you know, just stopping by for a little drink before . . . I must say, she is my favourite. She's out of sight . . . I think it's a mistake to have their breasts exposed. An error in theatrics. They should be wearing some thin negligee. Mystery . . .

BABE: *That's what turns me off to some of the hippie chicks. I guess I'm old fashioned enough to still want some femininity and expect a little mystery. But those chicks in Levis and scraggly hair really turn me off.*

I like chicks in Levis. My taste is like whoever approaches me, I think it's groovy.

Sounds pretty exhausting.

BABE: *You know what's a groovy word? Bell-wether: leader of a mindless crowd. That's what you are, Jim. The leader of a mindless crowd.*

Babe, that's what I mean. You got to learn to curb your tongue. I can see what it will be like. John would say, 'and then Babe said you know what you are Jim? The leader of a mindless crowd.' If you print that, John, I won't kill you, I'll haunt you. They all have minds. Maybe collectively . . . a crowd together really has no mind. Individually everybody does. They all have bitchin' minds. Like, I bet there's more philosophy in some sixteen-year-old chick's mind than you ever dreamed of in your whole cigarette. Some of those letters to those fan magazines are really lonely and deep and open. Some of them are bullshit. I don't read many, but some that I've read really knocked me out. Really open, sincere. Anyway, you got to learn to hold your tongue. Can you remember that?

BABE: *I'll remember that. I'll keep silent like deep water. Whenever I say anything from now on, it will be such a profundity that you guys will just fall out of your chairs.*

WAITRESS: *That will be $39.75.*

WNET-TV
CRITIQUE
Richard Goldstein
Spring 1969

This was the first interview after the Miami concert,
conducted in a television studio in New York.
The interviewer was Richard Goldstein, a writer for the
Village Voice who previously interviewed Jim
in 1968 for *New York* magazine. The interview
was a brief one, coupled with a live
performance by the Doors.

OK, let's talk about the Doors. They begin at U.C.L.A. where Morrison and Manzarek are enrolled in a Master's programme in film-making; they share a house in Venice, California, near the beach. Ray introduces his friends Krieger and Densmore to Jim's poetry; they begin to jam together at small clubs on the Sunset Strip and even in their early tapes there's a distinct bluesy feeling, which sometimes gets lost in the poetics but usually comes out in the rhythm, where it counts. Anyway, a huge record company signs them, then changes its mind, another company grabs them up and this time they record. Their first album sells more copies than My Weekly Reader; *they become superstars, able to leap tall groupies in a single bound, able to fill any hall in the western world. They garner as much publicity from their presence as they do from their music. This seems to put the authorities uptight but it delights the kids. It's like Jim Morrison once said: 'When you make your peace with authority you become an authority'. I interviewed the Doors when they were in town a few weeks ago and I'd like to run some of that tape for you now.*

JIM MORRISON: I think in a way rock concerts have always served a function. It gives a lot of people, with the same station in life, a chance to gather together and kind of assemble and just feel the sheer mass of them that exists, that the numbers . . .

RICHARD GOLDSTEIN: *I think that's a good point*

RAY MANZAREK: On the other hand you can take 10,000 people coming together and there's a sense of communion, a communal thing; we're all here together and there's no reason. A lot of energy is dissipated in the concert, but there's no reason that that same communal thing can't be taken out into the outside world and ideally, hopefully, that's what a rock, a good rock concert can do. People are together inside and they get outside into the parking lot and start driving home, and get into their homes. I hope they still realise that they're together – you know, they were together in the concert, and they're together in their homes, they're together in their schools, they're together on the street. And if the people can work that togetherness and keep that thing going, working it, and working it, eventually, everything's going to turn out alright.

You get a community feeling.

[Yeah]

The Interviews: Richard Goldstein

A contact high, so to speak . . . I once wrote a piece on you called The Shaman as Superstar *in which I suggested that rock musicians, rock heroes, perform a religious function for young people. Do you sometimes see your concerts as a sort of ritual?*

JIM MORRISON: It's a funny thing . . . I've read a little bit about shamanism. I haven't seen too much of it first hand, except you know, what we see with the music and that kind of thing, but in, er, tribes the shaman can be any age, can be an old man, or a young man, but the whole tribe, all ages, kind of try to push him into his trip and listen to him, irregardless [*sic*]. It was just a question of a certain psychological tendency in the individual.

What do you think the role is of say, a rock shaman in a time of social turmoil, with kids taking things into their own hands more or less.

JIM MORRISON: I don't think the shaman from what I've read, is really too interested in defining his role in society. He's just more interested in pursuing his own fantasies. If he became too self-conscious of a function, you know, I think it might tend to ruin his own inner trip.

Do you think that's why a lot of rock people have been reluctant to get involved in issue-oriented politics, you know, make statements on the school crisis and what have you?

JIM MORRISON: A lot of people just aren't interested in politics at all.

Well, as you go round the world, as you travel, through Europe and America, what do kids look for as far as projecting through you?

JOHN DENSMORE: Its funny – in Europe the kids were much more politically-oriented, you know. If we said anything politically they'd go into a furore. I mean they love it, especially anything against America, you know. If we just played they dug that too, but they really dug the political side of it, but in America it's just the opposite really. A lot of people at our concerts at least, they're sort of, it seems like they don't really come to hear us speak politics.

What do they come to hear?

JOHN DENSMORE: I think they come more for the religious experience.

How does that translate in terms of rhythm, riffs and things like that?

RAY MANZAREK: You really can't, because any rhythm, any riff, any sort of lyric is a release, you know, you're releasing yourself totally into whatever you happen to be playing at the moment.

How about in lyrics? What's the difference between a rock lyric and a poem?

RAY MANZAREK: Well, there's really no difference, you know.

213

Jim's book is the same as Jim's lyrics. I can read a page and I've heard him sing pretty much the same things. You know for him I don't think it's any difference at all – this is written poetry and what he does on stage is spoken poetry. His spoken poetry is very effective, although some poems read better than they speak, but for the most part, spoken poetry is much more effective.

JOHN DENSMORE: What we do sometimes is like we'll play a song and we'll play the structure of the song and then we'll get into a free part and we'll improvise musically and he'll improvise lyrically and that will probably be just straight poetry, you know, and then we'll get back into the form later.

It would naturally seem much more fluid than what you've got in the book then.

JIM MORRISON: A lot of our most interesting songs develop over a period of time playing night after night in clubs. We'd start out into a fairly basic song and then the music would settle into a kind of hypnotic river of sound which would leave me free to kind of make up anything that came into my head at the time. I like songs but that's the part of the performance that I enjoy the most, to pick up vibrations from the music and what's coming from the audience and, er, just kind of follow it wherever it goes.

How does that differ from when you write a poem?

JIM MORRISON: It's very similar. I think a lot of poetry is very close to music except when you write a poem often you just, you have to be in a state of mind that music can put you in, with its hypnotic quality that leaves you free, you know just to let the subconscious play itself out wherever it goes. I really admire poets who can get up with or without a microphone just in front of a group of people and start reciting their poetry. I really admire that. But I find the music gives me a kind of security and it makes it a lot easier to express myself or else, it's kind of hard just to read it dry. I wish I could, I'd like to work on that a little bit more.

I think that one of the trends which are pretty evident in rock now is that it's becoming demystified. The mystery is being extracted and we're getting very concerned with words like honest music, down-home music, and things like that, you know. How does this affect your stuff?

JIM MORRISON: I was talking about that this weekend, thinking a lot about it. I think the two basic types of music indigenous to this country are the black music, blues, and the kind of folk music that was brought over from Europe, I guess they call it country music or the kind of West Virginia High and Lonesome sound. Those are the two mainstreams of root American music, and there might be others around, but it looks like ten years ago what they called rock'n'roll was kind of a blending of those two forms. I guess what's happening now is that rock is kinda dying out and everyone's going back to their roots again. Some are going back into country and some are going back into basic blues. I guess in four or five years, the new generation's music will have a synthesis of those two elements and some third thing that will entire . . . maybe it'll be, it might rely heavily on electronics, er, tapes . . . I can kind of envision maybe one person with a lot of machines, tapes and electronic set-ups, singing or speaking and using machines.

I used to think that rock was progressing, you know, that there's a line from some point to another. But instead it's a wave, really, and there's a return to . . .

JIM MORRISON: That's why I like blues and jazz musicians, country musicians, they just keep on exploring their own music. Sometimes they're right on time and the public finds something in it that expresses the time, and sometimes they're out of favour, but I think for musicians and poets, artists in general, just to keep exploring their own field and if you're popular go with it, and if you go out of favour just keep doing it, you know.

The Lizard King

The week I interviewed Jim Morrison, the Doors were being banned from performing in St. Louis and Honolulu because of exhibitionism and drunkenness charges filed against Morrison following a concert in Miami – yet, it was the same week that Morrison finished writing a screenplay with poet Michael McClure and signed a contract with Simon and Schuster for his own first book of poetry.

Unlike the mythology, the music of the Doors remains a constant – a force which has not been so much an 'influence' in rock, but a monument. 'The music is your special friend.' Morrison sang in 'The Music's Over' and for millions, the music of the Doors is just that; just as the Beatles' 'Sgt. Pepper' renders a generation weak with nostalgia, so does the Doors' 'Light My Fire.' At the group's peak, in 1967–68, there was also a strident urgency about Morrison's music. 'We want the world and we want it now.'

Morrison was somewhat reluctant to be interviewed by Rolling Stone *at first, believing the publication's coverage of the Miami concert and aftermath had made him seem a clown. Finally he changed his mind and in sessions that rambled over more than a week and several neighbourhood drinking spots, he proved his manager Bill Siddons correct when Siddons said, 'Jim used to have a lot of little demons inside him . . . but I don't think he has so many anymore.' In other words, Morrison had mellowed, matured. Still he was playful – 'This is really a strange way to make a living, isn't it?' he said one day – but he was also trying to get people to take him seriously. All poets wish to be taken seriously, but many also have acted in a style that would seem to contradict or destroy this wish.*

The first session we met at the Doors' office (which is convenient to both the Elektra office and several topless clubs) and talked in a neighbourhood bar called the Palms. The idea was to get some lunch with the beer, but the cook was out for the day so it was just beer – with a small group of regulars scattered along the bar buying each other rounds and telling noisy stories in the background, while we sat at a small table nearby. There was no perceptible notice paid Morrison when he entered, and the full beard he had grown since Miami had little to do with it; he was a regular here, too.

JERRY HOPKINS: *How did you decide you were going to be a performer?*
JIM MORRISON: I think I had a suppressed desire to do something like this ever since I heard . . . y'see, the birth of rock'n'roll

coincided with my adolescence, my coming into awareness. It was a real turn-on, although at the time I could never allow myself to rationally fantasise about doing it myself. I guess all that time I was unconsciously accumulating inclination and listening. So when it finally happened, my subconscious had prepared the whole thing.

I didn't think about it. It was just there. I never did any singing. I never even conceived it. I thought I was going to be a writer or a sociologist, maybe write plays. I never went to concerts – one or two at most. I saw a few things on TV, but I'd never been part of it all. But I heard in my head a whole concert situation, with a band singing and an audience – a large audience. Those first five or six songs I wrote, I was just taking notes at a fantastic rock concert that was going on inside my head. And once I had written the songs, I had to sing them.

When was this?

About three years ago. I wasn't in a group or anything. I just got out of college and I went down to the beach. I wasn't doing much of anything. I was free for the first time. I had been going to school, constantly, for fifteen years. It was a beautiful hot summer, and I just started hearing songs. I think I still have the notebook with those songs written in it. This kind of mythic concert that I heard . . . I'd like to try and reproduce it sometime, either in actuality or on record. I'd like to reproduce what I heard on the beach that day.

Had you ever played any musical instrument?

When I was a kid I tried piano for a while, but I didn't have the discipline to keep up with it.

How long did you take piano?

Only a few months. I think I got to about the third-grade book.

Any desire now to play an instrument?

Not really. I play maracas. I can play a few songs on the piano. Just my own inventions, so it's not really music; it's noise. I can play one song. But it's got only two changes in it, two chords, so it's pretty basic stuff. I would really like to be able to play guitar, but I don't have the feeling for it. [*Pause*] You play any?

No . . .

I read a book you did – *The Hippie Papers*. It had some nice articles in it. I've thought of writing for the underground press, because I don't know anywhere else you can have an idea one day and see it in print almost immediately. I'd like to write a column for under-ground newspapers. Just reporting things I see. Not fiction, but reporting. Just trying to get accurate reports on things I witness – around L.A. especially. I guess I'm afraid of wasting a lot of good ideas on journalism. If I kept them in my head long enough they might really turn into something. Although there've been some good people writing as journalists – Dickens, Dostoevski . . . and of course Mailer is a contemporary journalist.

Mailer even turned out a novel, a chapter a month under deadline for Esquire . . .

And it's brilliant. *The American Dream.* Probably one of the best novels in the last decade.

It's interesting . . . a lot of good stuff is conceived specifically for newspapers and magazines, just as a lot of good music is conceived for records – all of which are disposable items, things which are available to just about anyone for very little money and later thrown away or traded in or gotten rid of pretty quickly. It's making several art forms very temporary . . .

That's why poetry appeals to me so much – because it's so eternal. As long as there are people, they can remember words and combinations of words. Nothing else can survive a holocaust, but poetry and songs. No one can remember an entire novel. No one can describe a film, a piece of sculpture, a painting. But so long as there are human beings, songs and poetry can continue.

When did you start writing poetry?

Oh, I think around the fifth or sixth grade I wrote a poem called 'The Pony Express'. That was the first I can remember. It was one of those ballad-type poems. I never could get it together, though. I always wanted to write, but I figured it'd be no good unless somehow the hand just took the pen and started moving without me really having anything to do with it. Like, automatic writing. But it just never happened. I wrote a few poems, of course.

Like 'Horse Latitudes' I wrote when I was in high school. I kept a lot of notebooks through high school and college, and then when I left school for some dumb reason – maybe it was wise – I threw them all away. There's nothing I can think of I'd rather have in my possession right now than those two or three lost notebooks. I was thinking of being hypnotised or taking sodium pentathol to try to remember, because I wrote in those books night after night. But maybe if I'd never thrown them away, I'd never have written anything original – because they were mainly accumulations of things that I'd read or heard, like quotes from books. I think if I'd never gotten rid of them I'd never have been free.

Do you have songs you like better than others?

I tell you the truth, I don't listen to the stuff much. There are songs I enjoy doing more in person than others. I like singing the blues – these free, long blues trips where there's no specific beginning or end. It just gets into a groove, and I can just keep making up things. And everybody's soloing. I like that kind of song rather than just a *song*. You know, just starting on a blues and just seeing where it takes us.

Improvisational trips . . .

Yeah. We needed another song for this album. We were racking our brains trying to think what song. We were in the studio, and so we started throwing out all these old songs. Blues trips. Rock classics. Finally we just started playing and we played for about an hour, and we went through the whole history of rock music – starting with blues, going through rock'n'roll, surf music, Latin, the whole thing. I call it 'Rock Is Dead.' I doubt if anybody'll ever hear it.

You were quoted recently as saying you thought rock was dead. Is this something you really believe?

It's like what we were talking about earlier in the movement back to the roots. The initial flash is over. The thing they call rock, what used to be called rock'n'roll – it got decadent. And then there was a rock revival sparked by the English. That went very far. It was articulate. Then it became self-conscious, which I think is the death of any movement. It became self-conscious, involuted and kind of incestuous. The energy is gone. There is no longer a belief.

I think that for any generation to assert itself as an aware human entity, it has to break with the past, so obviously the kids that are coming along next are not going to have much in common with what we feel. They're going to create their own unique sound. Things like wars and monetary cycles get involved too. Rock'n'roll probably could be explained by . . . it was after the Korean War was ended . . . and there was a psychic purge. There seemed to be a need for an underground explosion, like an eruption. So maybe after the Vietnam War is over – it'll probably take a couple of years maybe; it's hard to say – but it's possible that the deaths will end in a couple of years, and there will again be a need for a life force to express itself, to assert itself.

Do you feel you'll be part of it?

Yeah, but I'll probably be doing something else by then. It's hard to say. Maybe I'll be a corporation executive . . .

Have you ever thought of yourself in that role – seriously?

I kinda like the image. Big office. Secretary . . .

How do you see yourself? Poet? Rock Star? What?

I don't get too much feedback except what I read. I like to read things that are written about it. That's the only time I get any kind of feedback on the whole thing. Living in L.A., it's no big deal. It's an anonymous city, and I live an anonymous life. Our group never reached the mass phenomenon stage that some did, either; there never was the mass adulation. So it never really got to me much. I guess I see myself as a conscious artist plugging away from day to day, assimilating information. I'd like to get a theatre going of my own. I'm very interested in that now. Although I still enjoy singing.

A question you've been asked before, countless times: do you see yourself in a political role? I'm throwing a quote of yours back at you, in which you described the Doors as 'erotic politicians'.

It was just that I've been aware of the national media while growing up. They were always around the house, and so I started reading them. And so I became aware gradually, just by osmosis, of their style, their approach to reality. When I got into the music field, I was interested in securing kind of a place in that world, and so I was turning keys, and I just knew instinctively how to do it. They look for catchy phrases and quotes they can use for captions, something to base an article on to give it an immediate response. It's the kind of term that does mean something, but it's impossible to explain. If I tried to explain what it means to me, it would lose all its force as a catchword.

Deliberate media manipulation, right? Two questions come to me. Why did you pick that phrase over others? And do you think it's pretty easy to manipulate the media?

I don't know if it's easy, because it can turn on you. But, well, that was just one reporter, y'see. I was just answering his question. Since then a lot of people have picked up on it – that phrase – and have made it pretty heavy, but actually I was just . . . I knew the guy would use it, and I knew what the picture painted would be. I knew that a few key phrases is all anyone ever retains from an article. So I wanted a phrase that would stick in the mind.

I do think it's more difficult to manipulate TV and film than it is the press. The press has been easy for me in a way, because I am biased toward writing, and I understand writing and the mind of writers; we are dealing with the same medium, the printed word. So that's been fairly easy. But television and films are much more difficult, and I'm still learning. Each time I go on TV I get a little more relaxed and a little more able to communicate openly, and control it. It's an interesting process.

Does this explain your fascination with film?

I'm interested in film because to me it's the closest approximation in art that we have to the actual flow of consciousness, in both dream life and in the everyday perception of the world.

You're getting more involved in film all the time . . .

Yeah, but there's only one we've completed – *Feast of Friends*, which was made at the end of a spiritual, cultural renaissance that's just about over now. It was like what happened at the end of the plague in Europe that decimated half the population. People danced, they wore colourful clothing. It was a kind of incredible springtime. It'll happen again, but it's over, and the film was made at the end of it.

I think of one part of the film, a performance sequence, in which you're flat on your back, still singing . . . which represents how theatrical you've gotten in your performance. How did this theatricality develop? Was it a conscious thing?

I think in a club, histrionics would be a little out of place, because the room is too small and it would be a little grotesque. In a large concert situation, I think it's just . . . necessary, because it gets to be more than just a musical event. It turns into a little bit of a spectacle. And it's different every time. I don't think any one performance is like any other. I can't answer that very well. I'm not too conscious of what's happening. I don't like to be too objective about it. I like to let each thing happen – direct it a little consciously, maybe, but just kind of follow the vibrations I get in each particular circumstance. We don't plan theatrics. We hardly ever know which set we'll play.

You mentioned that there were certain songs you liked performing over others, those which allow you some room for improvisation. I assume you mean pieces like 'The End' and 'The Music's Over' . . .

Once they got on record, they became very ritualised and static. Those were kind of constantly changing free-form pieces but once we put them on record, they just kind of stopped. They were kind of at the height of their effect anyway, so it didn't really matter. No . . . I mean the kind of songs where the musicians just start jamming. It starts off with a rhythm, and you don't know how it's going to be or really what it's about, until it's over. That sort I enjoy best.

When you're writing material, do you consciously differentiate between a poem, something for print . . . and a song lyric, something to be sung?

To me a song comes with the music, a sound or rhythm first, then I make up words as fast as I can just to hold onto the feel – until actually the music and the lyric come almost simultaneously. With a poem, there's not necessarily any music . . .

But usually a sense of rhythm, though . . .

Right. Right. A sense of rhythm and, in that sense, a kind of music. But a song is more primitive. Usually has a rhyme and a basic meter, whereas a poem can go anywhere.

Well, who provides this musical line that you hear when you're writing? The band? Or is this something you hear inside your head?

Well, most songs I've written just came. I'm not a very prolific songwriter. Most of the songs I've written I wrote in the very beginning, about three years ago. I just had a period when I wrote a lot of songs.

In the first three albums, writer credit in every song goes to the Doors, as opposed to individuals. But I understand that in the next album individual writers will be listed. Why?

In the beginning, I wrote most of the songs, the words and music. On each successive album, Robby [Krieger] contributed more songs. Until finally on this album it's almost split between us.

A lot of the songs in the beginning, me or Robby would come in with a basic idea, words and melody. But then the whole arrangement and actual generation of the piece would happen night after night, day after day, either in rehearsals or in clubs. When we became a concert group, a record group, and when we were contracted to provide so many albums a year, so many singles every six months, that natural, spontaneous, generative process wasn't given a chance to happen as it had in the beginning. We actually had to create songs in the studio. What started to happen was Robby or I would just come in with a song and the arrangement already completed in our minds, instead of working it out slowly.

Do you think your work has suffered because of this?

Yeah. If we did nothing but record, it probably would be all right. But we do other things, too, so there's not the time to let things happen as they should. Our first album, which a lot of people like, has a certain unity of mood. It has an intensity about it, because it was the first album we'd recorded. And we did it in a couple of weeks. That's all it took to get it down. It came after almost a year of almost total performance, every night. We were really fresh and intense and together.

This was at Elektra, of course. But you'd been signed to Columbia earlier. What happened there?

Well, it was just . . . in the beginning I'd written some songs and Ray [Manzarek] and his brothers had a band, Rick and the Ravens, and they had a contract with World-Pacific. They'd tried to get a couple of singles out and nothing happened. Well, they still had their contract to do a few more sides and we'd gotten together by then, and so we went in and cut six sides in about three hours. At that time, Robby wasn't with the group. But John [Densmore] was the drummer. Ray was on piano, I was singing and his two brothers . . . one played harp, one played guitar, and there was a girl bass player – I can't remember her name.

So what we got was an acetate demo, and we had three copies pressed, right? I took them around everywhere I could possibly think of . . . going to the record companies. I hit most of them . . . just going in the door and telling the secretary what I wanted. Sometimes they'd say leave your number, and sometimes they'd let you in to talk to someone else. The reception game. At Columbia they became interested. The first person anyone meets when they come to Columbia is the head of talent research and development. Actually, the first person is his secretary. They liked it.

This was Billy James . . .

Yeah, and a girl named Joan Wilson was his secretary. She called me a few days later and said he'd like to talk to us. We got a contract with Columbia for six months, during which they were going to produce so many sides. Having that contract was kind of an incentive for us to stay together. It turned out that no one was interested in producing us at that time, though, so we asked to get out of the contract.

Before the six months had elapsed?

Yeah. We knew we were onto something, and we didn't want to get held to some kind of contract at the last moment. By now we'd realised Columbia wasn't where it was at as far we were concerned. It was kind of fortunate, really. We've had a good relationship with the company we're with now. They're good people to work with.

Well, how'd that come about . . . with Elektra?

Elektra at that time was very new to the rock field. . . . They had Love, and early Butterfield stuff. But Butterfield was still into blues, into the folk bag. Love was their first rock group and actually represented their first singles potential. They had been mainly an album label. After they signed Love, the president of the company heard us play at the Whisky. I think he told me once he didn't like it. The second or third night . . . he kept coming back, and finally everyone was convinced we'd be very successful. So he signed us up.

I've been told or I read somewhere that after the Columbia episode, you were somewhat reluctant to sign with anybody else.

I can't remember exactly. The people said that everyone in town was trying to sign us up, but it wasn't really true. In fact, Jac Holzman's may have been the only concrete offer we had. We may have made him come up with the best deal possible, but there *was* no question but what we weren't that much in demand.

You said the first LP went easily . . .

Fast. We started almost immediately, and some of the songs took only a few takes. We'd do several takes just to make sure we couldn't do a better one. It's also true that on the first album they don't want to spend as much. The group doesn't either, because the groups pay for the production of an album. That's part of the advance against royalties. You don't get any royalties until you've paid the cost of the record album. So the group and the record company weren't taking a chance on the cost. So for economic reasons and just because we were ready, it went very fast.

Subsequent albums have been harder?

Harder and cost a lot more. But that's the natural thing. When we make a million dollars on each album and hit singles come from those albums, we can afford it. It's not always the best way, though.

In your early biographies, it says your parents are dead – yet your family is really very much alive. Why the early story?

I just didn't want to involve them. It's easy enough to find out personal details if you really want them. When we're born we're all footprinted and so on. I guess I said my parents were dead as some kind of joke. I have a brother, too, but I haven't seen him in about a year. I don't see any of them. This is the most I've ever said about this.

Getting back to your film, then, there's some of the most incredible footage I've ever seen of an audience rushing a performer. What do you think in situations like that?

It's just a lot of fun *[Laughter]*. It actually looks a lot more exciting than it really is. Film compresses everything. It packs a lot of energy into a small . . . anytime you put a form on reality, it's going to look more intense. Truthfully, a lot of times it was very exciting, a lot of fun. I enjoy it or I wouldn't do it.

You said the other day that you like to get people up out of their seats, but not intentionally create a chaos situation . . .

It's never gotten out of control, actually. It's pretty playful, really. We have fun, the kids have fun, the cops have fun. It's kind of a weird triangle. We just think about going out to play good music. Sometimes I'll extend myself and work people up a little bit, but usually we're out there trying to make good music, and that's it.

What do you mean, you'll sometimes extend yourself . . . work the people up a bit?

Let's just say I was testing the bounds of reality. I was curious to see what would happen. That's all it was: just curiosity.

226

What did you do to test the bounds?

Just push a situation as far as it'll go.

And yet you don't feel at any time that things got out of control?

Never.

Even in your film . . . when it shows cops throwing kids back off the stage as fast as they're diving onto it? That doesn't represent some loss of control?

You have to look at it logically. If there were no cops there, would anybody try to get onstage? Because what are they going to do when they get there? When they get onstage, they're just very peaceful. They're not going to do anything. The only incentive to charge the stage is because there's a barrier. If there was no barrier, there'd be no incentive. That's the whole thing. I firmly believe that. No incentive, no charge. Action-reaction. Think of the free concerts in the parks. No action, no reaction. No stimulus, no response. It's interesting, though, because the kids get a chance to test the cops. You see cops today, walking around with their guns and uniforms, and the cop is setting himself up like the toughest man on the block, and everyone's curious about exactly what would happen if you challenged him. What's he going to do? I think it's a good thing, because it gives the kids a chance to test the authority.

There are a number of cities where . . . like, you were busted for obscenity in New Haven. In Phoenix it was something else . . .

I would say in most cases the only time we get into trouble is, like, if a person is just walking down a busy street and for no reason at all just took their clothes off and kept on walking . . . you can do anything as long as it's in tune with the forces of the universe, nature, society, whatever. If it's in tune, if it's working, you can do anything. If for some reason you're on a different track from other people you're around, it's going to jangle everybody's sensibilities. And they're either going to walk away or put you down for it. So it's just a case of getting too far out for them, or everybody's on a different trip that night and nothing comes together. As long as everything's connecting and coming together, you can get away with murder.

There is a quote attributed to you. It appears in print a lot. It goes: 'I'm interested in anything about revolt, disorder, chaos . . .'

'. . . especially activity that appears to have no meaning.'

Right. That one. Is this another example of media manipulation? Did you make that one up for a newspaper guy?

Yes, definitely. But it's true, too. Who isn't fascinated with chaos? More than that, though, I am interested in activity that has no

227

meaning, and all I mean by that is free activity. Play. Activity that has nothing in it except just what it is. No repercussions. No motivation. Free . . . activity. I think there should be a national carnival, much the same as Mardi Gras in Rio. There should be a week of national hilarity . . . a cessation of all work, all business, all discrimination, all authority. A week of total freedom. That'd be a start. Of course, the power structure wouldn't really alter. But someone offthe streets – I don't know how they'd pick him, at random perhaps – would become president. Someone else would become vice-president. Others would be senators, congressmen, on the Supreme Court, policemen. It would just last for a week and then go back to the way it was. I think we need it. Yeah. Something like that.

This may be insulting, but I have the feeling I'm being put on . . .

A little bit. But I don't know. People would have to be real for a week. And it might help the rest of the year. There would have to be some form or ritual to it. I think something like that is really needed.

There are a few words that recur in your dialogue. One is the word 'ritual'. What's that mean to you?

It's kind of like human sculpture. In a way it's like art, because it gives form to energy, and in a way it's a custom or a repetition, an habitually recurring plan or pageant that has meaning. It pervades everything. It's like a game.

Is there a ritual or a sense of game about what you and/or the Doors as a group do?

Yeah, it's a ritual in the sense that we use the same props and the same people and the same forms time after time after time. Music is definitely a ritual. But I don't think this is really clarifying ritual or adding anything to it.

Do you see yourself going more toward print?

That's my greatest hope. That's always been my dream.

Who turned you on to poetry?

I guess it was whoever taught me to speak, to talk. Really. I guess it was the first time I learned to talk. Up until the advent of language, it was touch – non-verbal communication.

What do you think of journalists?

I could be a journalist. I think the interview is the new art form. I think the self-interview is the essence of creativity. Asking yourself questions and trying to find answers. The writer is just answering a series of unuttered questions.

You've twice said you think you successfully manipulated the press. How much of this interview was manipulated?

You can't ever get around the fact that what you say could possibly turn up in print sometime, so you have that in the back of your mind. I've tried to forget it.

Is there some other area you'd like to get into?

How about . . . feel like discussing alcohol? Just a short dialogue. No long rap. Alcohol as opposed to drugs?

Okay. Part of the mythology has you playing the role of a heavy juicer.

On a very basic level, I love drinking. But I can't see drinking just milk or water or Coca-Cola. It just ruins it for me. You have to have wine or beer to complete a meal *[Long pause]*.

That's all you want to say? [Laughter]

Getting drunk . . . you're in complete control up to a point. It's your choice, every time you take a sip. You have a lot of small choices. It's like . . . I guess it's the difference between suicide and slow capitulation. . . .

What's that mean?

I don't know, man. Let's go next door and get a drink.

Z I G Z A G
John Tobler
Autumn 1970

John Tobler, one of Britain's most prolific rock writers,
interviewed Jim at the Isle of Wight Festival.
This was the Doors' second visit to England, taken
during a break in the Miami trial. The interview
is one of the briefest in the present collection, yet it
clearly shows the doubts that Jim held regarding any
talk about 'revolution' in America.

JOHN TOBLER: *I've discovered a book on sale at this festival called* The Doors Song Book, *which appears to be a pirated version of all the words off all the albums, including the new one. What do you reckon about that?*

JIM MORRISON: Well, I don't mind if they've got all the words spelt right. A lot of the time they really screw up the meaning, just one word or one semi-colon can ruin the whole thing.

Do you approve of having the lyrics on the back of your album or on the inside sleeve, because in England, two of them have had the lyrics and three haven't. Do you think it makes a difference? We didn't have the words to 'The Unknown Soldier' for instance.

Yeah, they really got botched up. I don't think it matters. I don't think it's necessary but . . .

You don't mind that somebody's making some bread out of your words?

No, what harm could it do?

Is this the first festival of this sort you've played?

Yes, it is.

How do you find it? I mean the chaos and the devastation and the . . . you know, it's OK in here, but have you been outside?

Well, it's kind of hard walking around out there. I did get around back around the camp-sites a little bit, but this one seems to be pretty well organised for such a huge event. I didn't have such a good time last night, because I had to perform, and I'd just gotten off the plane. But tonight, I came back, and I can see why people like it. I think all these people who say that huge festivals are over and dead, I think they're wrong. I think they're going to become increasingly significant in the next three or four or five years.

When I talked to some cats who came back from Woodstock, like Clive Selwood [London's Elektra representative], he said it was terrible. You know, the sheer inability to cope with the multitudes, and now they've made the film, and everyone's saying 'Wow! Beautiful revolution'.

I'm sure that these things get highly romanticised but I was kind of that opinion myself when I saw the film. It seemed like a bunch of young parasites, being kind of spoonfed this three or four days of . . . well you know what I mean. They looked like victims and dupes of a culture, rather than anything, but I think that may have been sour grapes, because I wasn't there, not even as a spectator, so I think that even though they are a mess, and even though they are not what they pretend to be, some free celebration of a young culture, it's still better than nothing. And I'm sure that some of the people take away a kind of myth back to the city with them, and it'll affect them.

I take it that you don't believe in this sudden, miraculous revolution that's being spoken about as if we're all going to go back to London and take over.

That would be unreal to me. I don't want to say too much because I haven't studied politics that much, really. It just seems that you have to be in a constant state of revolution, or you're dead. There always has to be a revolution, it has to be a constant thing, not something that's going to change things, and that's it, you know, the revolution's going to solve everything. It has to be every day.

I figure that you've got to convince people gradually to change, not to say 'Pow, we're coming in!' like the Black Panthers.

There have to be Black Panthers too. They have to change too, to become leopards some day, right?

You played mostly tracks off your first two albums last night. Why was that, because you thought we'd know those better?

No, we knew them better.

You don't do many gigs at that rate then?

Yeah, we do, but never anything like this. I don't think that our particular music style holds up very well in a huge outdoor event. I think that the particular kind of magic that we can breed when we do, when it works, works best in a small theatre.

Like the last time you came to England?

Yeah, that was beautiful, I think.

Yeah, right, I saw the last set; you know, when the dawn was breaking on the Saturday, and it was incredible.

I think that was one of the best concerts we've ever done.

I was talking to the guy this morning who made the film, and I said –

Which one?

Geoffrey Canon – he's a writer for The Guardian *– and he said that they were trying to put over the immediacy of rock, rather than the Doors, and I said well, I think you should have been trying to put over the Doors, because the sound recording was really shitty, you know.*

However, I thought the film was very exciting. To get it on national television, I think that's incredible. The thing is, the guys that made the film had a thesis of what their film was going to be, before we even came over. We were going to be the political rock group, and it gave them the chance to whip out some of their anti-American sentiments, which they thought we were going to give them, and so they had their whole film before we came over. But I still think they made a very exciting film.

You know, when you were at the Roundhouse, there was something . . . It was amazing, all those people sitting there. It was so crowded it was much worse than this, because it was an enclosed space, and there was a queue of two thousand people waiting to get in at two o'clock in the morning. A ridiculous scene. Why haven't you been here since then?

I guess we've been too busy, and actually, there didn't seem to be that much demand. I mean, we couldn't go back to the Roundhouse; it would have to be a step forward, and there didn't seem to be any real, uh . . .

No. Well, the Roundhouse is no longer an auditorium in the same way. Oh Calcutta's on there, right?

Right.

That seems strange.

They put sort of terraced seating in not long after you came.

Well, that was a beautiful scene two years ago, at the Roundhouse where it's kind of a penny theatre, you know.

Right . . . It's the kind of thing one remembers for years and years, which is why I'd have expected an earlier return.

That's the reason. We were busy, and also there just didn't seem to be any real demand for it. What's the name of the magazine you guys put out?

Zigzag.

I've seen it. I'd like to start a magazine, newspaper thing in L.A. sometime. The trouble is, if you try and do it to sell copies, and get the advertising and all that, then you can't, uh . . .

Well, you certainly lose a lot of your enthusiasm when you start getting involved in business hustles. Anyway, wouldn't L.A. be rather a difficult market, with so many publications?

Well, that's it. I would only do it if I could finance it myself, so I wouldn't have to advertise. You know those little magazines, one issue things, the Surrealists and Dadaists used to put out? Manifestos, and all that?

Yeah, right.

Hey look. An actual movie. *[As Jimi Hendrix is filmed going up the backstage ramp followed by a man struggling with an enormous camera.]* Hey that's beautiful. Looks like a priest.

Do you think in view of what you've done that you will do a tour now?

Well, we had planned one . . . we had planned to do it after this, eight or nine places in Europe, including Italy and Switzerland and Paris, places like that, but I have to go back to this trial in

Miami. I'm in the middle of that, so it blew the whole trip.

That is such a drag, as far as we here are concerned.

I thought it was going to be, but it's actually a very fascinating thing to go through. A thing you can observe.

I talked to Jac Holzman [of Elektra], and he said that it was going on so long now that perhaps nothing would ever be done about it, because it would go to appeals and appeals and appeals, but the trouble is if it keeps you in a position where you can't get out of the country for too long, it's a drag for us here.

I think maybe we'll come back next Spring, March, April. That's a good time of year.

That would be good. Are you happy with the live album?

Yeah, I like it.

We haven't heard it yet.

It's just about to be released here. I think it's a true document of one of our good concerts. It's not insanely good, but it's a true portrait of what we usually do on a good night. I think you'll like it.

Well, I've really dug all the others. I heard that your favourite album was The Soft Parade. *Is that right?*

Oh, I don't know. I guess I don't have a favourite. Well, let's see, I think my favourite, beside the live one, is *Morrison Hotel.*

That's very good. That was getting back to the first two, perhaps, it seemed to me. Was that . . .

Just in the respect that we didn't use any other musicians on it, except the bass player.

Lonnie Mack –

But it wasn't a conscious attempt to get back to anything.

No, but it was publicised a bit like that here, which is perhaps unfair, because the first album is an epic. I'm literally on my third copy of it, I wore out two.

Yeah? You know, that's terrible, that's like a novelist's first novel, and no one ever lets him forget it. Why don't you write 'em like *Look Homeward Angel* anymore?

No, you're certainly progressing, aren't you? I mean, I thought Morrison Hotel *was a knock out, whereas* The Soft Parade *disappointed me in places.*

It kinda got out of control, and it took too long in making, spread over about nine months, and just got out of hand. There was no, uh . . . an album should be like a book of stories strung together, some kind of unified feeling and style about it, and that's what that one lacks.

Are you happy with Elektra?

235

Yeah, it's been a great relationship.

I'm an Elektra freak. I've got about seventy Elektra albums.

Well, now that it's become part of a large corperation, it'll be interesting to see if the label gets better, or if they kinda get . . . or if it gets assimilated. Hopefully, it might give them the chance not to worry about the tedium of the popular field, and do the thing that they do best, which is classical, experimental electronic things, giving a chance to people that haven't had really a chance to be commercially successful in their own times. Maybe this will give them a chance to get back to that.

Which is what they first became known for.

I think with us it was just really a freak. They've never repeated that.

Jac Holzman saw you when he went to see Love playing somewhere, didn't he? That was the story.

Right. They had Love, and someone associated with them brought someone in to see us, and that's . . . yeah, that's actually it. Because Love was the popular underground group in L.A. at that time, and we figured, well, if they went on Elektra, it must be a good label.

And then you got famous, and Love didn't.

Yeah. In a way that's true. I think it was sad about Love, they were incredible . . . well, it's really Arthur Lee, I suppose because . . . although the first Love group was a very, very great group. But I don't think they were willing to travel, and to go through all the games and numbers that you have to do to get it out to a large number of people. If they'd done that, I think they could have been as big as anyone. And someday they will.

Right. Thanks very much for your time.

Good luck.

C I R C U S
Salli Stevenson
Winter 1970

Salli Stevenson was a freelance writer in Los Angeles
when she met Jim in October, between the Miami trial
and sentencing, when he was living temporarily in the
Hyatt House Hotel on the Sunset Strip, sharing a suite
of rooms with his pal Babe Hill. The interview was
conducted on October 14th, transcribed the next day,
and given to Jim on the 16th for editing; he removed
some references to the trial which might have been
considered legally damaging should he be found guilty
and subsequently filed an appeal. Salli remembers the
interview, conducted at the Doors' office, as being 'very
businesslike until we got to the Phone Booth'. After that
it was 'outrageous', she says, but by then the tape
recorder had been put away.
The interview appeared in two instalments, in
December 1970 and January 1971,
in *Circus* magazine.

The Lizard King

PART I

No matter what your individual concept of hell is, it is always a comforting thought to enter, if indeed you must, in the company of friends who may on a lucky chance, James Bond-like, pull you out at that last desperate second before the master engulfs your spirit forever. Hell: how do you visualise it? The very concept of its corporality is elusive, fascinating and as frightening as the ruler of its dominions. The physical entity has come down to us on canvases too numerous to mention, all exploding fire and brimstone, revolt and desolation. Its potentate flashes across the medieval consciousness of our minds with cloven hooves, horns and a pitchfork, the better to roast us as so many marshmallows over the hot coals of what later centuries have suggested is our own paranoia.

That was the image we poor puritans were blessed with. Satan was our boogeyman, used to scare nasty children on dark nights and then . . . he became fashionable, a spirit to be glorified by public and press alike. The ultimate modish embodiment was personified in satanist Mick Jagger and demonic Jim Morrison, the American sexist devil of the late sixties.

Of Jim's 'Image' nothing remains to be said, for prior releases, journalistic meanderings and performances have spelled it out in clinicalised, explicit reams. The fact that his latest escapade landed him asunder of the law last summer in Miami was something else.

It was almost four o'clock when Kurt Inghan (our photographer) and I met Risa, friend and PR girl, and sallied forth to see Jim for the first of what was to be roughly two days in the life of. The office, an ex-antique shop on Santa Monica Blvd., is California stucco browns and golds. The fact that it is perpetual dusk inside blinds you to the presence of a very quiet Jim, sans paunch, sitting in a corner behind a desk. His smile is slow, genial, more in his eyes and in view of the ringing phones and takin' care of business voices he suggests that we try taping in the garden which features a minute pool with four frying sized gold fish, a distinct change from the lizards and snakes you half expect. Risa inquires after the crocodile only to find that that particular pool resident is late, great and gone which delights me no end. Lizards are passable, but crocs don't do much for my frazzled stomach and we are all just a bit edgy about confronting the 'Image'. Jim asks for a cigarette explaining that he only smokes when nervous.

The Interviews: Salli Stevenson

SALLI STEVENSON: *Your latest album has received some rather harsh criticism, not only because it was another live album among the many released, but because of the lack of polish attributed to it by many critics. How did it come about and why the seeming lack of practice?*

JIM MORRISON: The *Live* album was condensed from about 24 hours of taped concerts that we did over approximately a year's period of time, starting with the Aquarius Theater in August 1969. We thought we might have one that night. We did two sets, but when we listened to it in the studio we found that it didn't really add up to a very good album. It was a good evening, but on tape it didn't sound that good. So we recorded seven or eight other concerts and listened to all of it and cut it down. I think it's a fairly true document of what the band sounds like on a fairly good night. It's not the best we can do and it's certainly not the worst. It's a true document of an above average evening. I like 'The Celebration', though it's not a great version of that piece, but I'm glad we went ahead and put it out, because I doubt if we would have ever put it on a record otherwise because it's a couple of years old. We tried to do it at the time we were doing *Waiting For The Sun* and it just didn't seem to make it in the studio, so we used one piece out of it, 'Not To Touch The Earth'. If we hadn't put it on a live album, we would have just shelved it forever. I'm glad that we did it even in the imperfect form in which it exists. It's better than if we had never done it. As far as the lack of practice . . . I think most of it is pretty professional. There are a few cuts that were done for the first time on stage, that we really hadn't worked with that much, that have flaws in them . . . but I don't think it's significant. People don't realise how different playing live is from recording. You work for days to get an instrumental track and then work for hours to get a vocal. Of course in a live thing, it's just that one shot. Basically the music has gotten progressively better, tighter and more professional . . . more interesting.

How then do you explain what appears to be a decline in your musical inventiveness over the last year or so? When you first started out, you were the great revolutionary hope of America and now the group seems to have mellowed.

Three years ago, if you remember, there was a great renaissance of spirit and emotion tied up with revolutionary sentiment. When things didn't change overnight, I think people resented the fact that we were just still around doing good music.

What about the deaths of Janis and Jimi. They went through the same period . . .

241

I think that that great creative burst of energy that happened three or four years ago was hard to sustain for the sensitive artists. I guess they might be dissatisfied with anything except 'the heights'. When reality stops fulfilling their inner visions, they get depressed.

RISA: *How do you think you'll die?*

I hope at about age 120 with a sense of humour and a nice comfortable bed. I wouldn't want anybody around. I'd just want to drift quietly off, but I'm still holding out. I think it's very possible that science has a chance in our lifetime to conquer death.

There are many people who believe in reincarnation and spirits. If medical science were to do that, what would happen to their spirit world?

They'd just have to fend for themselves. Leave us poor immortals alone.

I take it you don't believe in Karma or reincarnation or the occult beliefs?

No, not really, but since I don't have anything else to replace it with, I listen to everything. I don't say no.

What do you believe in then?

We evolved from snakes and I used to see the universe as a mammoth peristaltic snake. I used to see all the people and objects and landscapes as little pictures on the facets of their skins. I think the peristaltic motion is the basic life movement and even your basic unicellular structures have this same motion. It's swallowing, digestion, the rhythms of sexual intercourse.

It's been said that you've been on a superstar, super-ego trip. Has this affected you or your friends, or your relations with the band?

That's a complex one. Obviously you don't really talk about those things with people. I don't think it was that bad. I never noticed it too much except when I read magazine articles, but living in a town like L.A. you don't notice those images. People here are pretty blasé about things like that.

How about the magazines?

Actually I've always liked the things I've read. Of course it was about me. Usually you are most interested in yourself and people that you know. But . . . they were concentrating on my progenitive organ too much and weren't paying attention to the fact that I was a fairly healthy young male specimen who also had other than your usual arms, legs, ribs, thorax, eyes . . . but a cerebellum . . . your completely equipped human being with the head, sensitivity, the full equipment.

KURT: *For a while there was a cycle in pop stardom where people looked up to pop stars for their answers, forgetting that pop stars are people too.*

Now they seem to have come from idols to heroes.
Using the definition that a hero is someone you can reach out to and an idol is someone unreachable, do you consider yourself an idol or a hero?
A hero is someone who rebels or seems to rebel against the facts of existence and seems to conquer them. Obviously that can only work at moments. It can't be a lasting thing. That's not saying that people shouldn't keep trying to rebel against the facts of existence. Someday, who knows, we might conquer death, disease and war.
What about you, though . . .
I think of myself as an intelligent, sensitive human being with the soul of a clown, which always forces me to blow it at the most important moments.
If you had it to do over?
I'm not denying that I've had a good time these last three or four years. I've met a lot of interesting people and seen things in a short space of time that I probably would not have run into in twenty years of living. I can't say that I regret it. If I had it to do over, I think I would have gone for the quiet, undemonstrative artist, plodding away in his own garden.
When you were at U.C.L.A., you were involved in theatre and with that background you joined a band. Have your visions for the band become a reality?
Initially, I didn't start out to be a member of a band. I wanted to make films, write plays, books. When I found myself in a band, I wanted to bring some of these ideas into it. We never did much with it, though . . . it would take a long volume of prose to answer that with any degree of candour or truth. So, I think you're going to have to wait until I can get to work and write down what I really feel about that. It's too deep to cover in this amount of time and I wouldn't even want to give a short answer, because that's the most interesting question of all. I'm already working on it really, between interviews.
    I like interviews . . . it's similar to answering questions on a witness stand. It's that strange area where you try and pin down something that happened in the past and try honestly to remember what you were thinking about, what you were trying to do. It's a crucial mental exercise. An interview will often give you a chance to confront your mind with questions which to me is what art is all about. It's a form of self-interview in which you pose yourself questions and try to come up with a reasonable answer. An inter-view also gives you the chance to try and eliminate all of those space fillers. All they do is if you can't think of an accurate answer you just 'kind of, you know, ahh, what I mean'.

The Lizard King

KURT: *But everybody does it.*

I know. But you should not. Doctors, lawyers, scientists, good writers usually do. You'll notice that their conversation is much less vague than what you run up against with other people. It may be full of obscurities of its own kind, but you should try to be explicit, accurate, to the point . . . no bullshit. I like the interview form and I think it's going to become an increasingly important art form. It has antecedants in the confession box, debating and cross examination. Once you say something, you can't really retract it. It's too late. It's a very existential moment.

KURT: *Have you seen Alice Cooper or the Stooges?*

I haven't heard them. I've just read a few things about them . . . sounds great. I like people that shake other people up and make them uncomfortable.

Speaking of being uncomfortable, what's happening with the trial?

I had a six week trial and it was very interesting. The felony rap was dismissed and I'm still stuck with the two misdemeanours which could add up to eight months in jail. I'm admitting the charge of public profanity, but I'm denying the exposure charge. We're going to appeal that for as long as it takes to get it dismissed. It may take another year or two, I think it was more of a political than a sexual scandal. They picked on the erotic aspect, because there would have been no political charge they could have brought against me. It was too amorphous.

I really think that it was a lifestyle that was on trial more than any specific incident. Anyway, I go back to court on October 30th. *[Editor's note: This interview was conducted a few days before the trial.]* At that time there will be a sentence directed. The maximum would be eight months and a fine. However, whatever the sentence would be, even if it were suspended and there was a probation of some kind, we would still go ahead and appeal the conviction. The public profanity misdemeanour could be very easily dismissed because the Supreme Court has recently ruled that in a theatrical performance, not just theatrical performances, but in most other situations, the first amendment guarantees freedom of expression. That conviction would automatically be held unconstitutional. On the exposure charge we're maintaining innocence. Since the prosecution didn't come up with any real proof, we'll just appeal it and take it to a higher court. So I wouldn't go to jail immediately . . . I don't think.

It was a very interesting trial. I'd never actually seen the judicial system in action, the progress of a trial from the first day to the last. Being the defendant I had to be there for every day and it was fasci-

244

nating . . . very educational. I wouldn't have chosen to have gone through the experience, but while it was happening all I could do was watch.

PART II

Sitting, watching and waiting for a possible doom factor to happen with no way to halt it is a gut-wrenching, nerve-racking experience. Then the waiting was over, Jim Morrison faced Judge Murray Goodman in Miami.
   'You are a person graced with a talent, admired by many of your peers. Man tends to imitate that which he admires and those gifted with the ability to lead and influence others should strive to bring out the best, and not the worst in his admirers.' With that speech, Judge Goodman meted out the sentence for profanity and indecent exposure. Jim received six months, almost the maximum, and his bail was raised from $5,000 to $50,000. He is appealing the charge which could take up to three years and if successful, it is certain that he will have to serve no time at all. If the appeal fails he will probably serve a maximum of two months.

I was quite relieved that I wasn't taken into the jail and booked. They could have done it easily. I feel quite free for the first time in a year and a half. We're going to fight the sentence until it is wiped clean off the records. The appeal motion will first have to go to the Circuit Court in Florida and if it doesn't pass muster there, it will go to the State Court and eventually to the Supreme Court. If they accept it, there will be a final decision then.
   On what factors is the appeal to be based?
   The judge's attitude seemed to be that he was trying to prosecute me to the limits of the law. That will be one of our appeals, that I didn't really receive a fair trial because of judicial prejudice. For example, he limited the defence witnesses to the exact number that the prosecution had and he would allow no evidence regarding the contemporary community standards as, for example, taking the jury to see Woodstock and Hair and other current movies and plays that were showing in Miami at the time. These were two examples of his rigidity and lack of fairness in our opinion. The big charge, which was indecent exposure, was not conclusively proven in six weeks of testimony. There were ten to twelve thousand people there at the performance and countless cameras. The prosecution was not able to come up with one picture, one photograph of exposure.

The Lizard King

I understand that your attorney made a direct appeal for mercy to the bench at your sentence date. What was it, and in your opinion, did the judge take that into consideration?

Max stated that he'd known me for four or five years and that he knew me to be a good man who had contributed some important works to society and most likely would continue to contribute. He stated that the mode of expression used to communicate thoughts that I had at Miami, was common in today's context and that it wasn't of evil intent. As to the other charge, there was no proof. But it seemed that the judge had already decided what he was going to do. His mind was made up prior to Max's bench appeal.

What was the state of mind you had that got you into this whole Miami mess in the first place?

I think I was just fed up with the image that had been created around me, which I sometimes consciously, most of the time unconsciously cooperated with. It just got too much for me to really stomach and so I just put an end to it in one glorious evening. I guess what it boiled down to was that I told the audience that they were a bunch of fucking idiots to be members of an audience. What were they doing there anyway. The basic message was . . . realise that you're not really here to listen to a bunch of songs by some fairly good musicians. You're here for something else. Why not admit it and do something about it.

You did the Isle of Wight . . .

That was during the trial. I flew over from Miami, arrived in London and drove to a little airport, took a small plane to the Isle of Wight and then we drove right to the concert. By the time I went on, I don't think I'd had any sleep in 36 hours. I wasn't really quite at my best . . . my peak of physical condition. I don't think it would have mattered that much anyway. The performance during that period would probably have been about the same anyway.

What about the mildly negative attitudes of the British newspapers?

Let's put it this way. We were not the highlight of the festivities. We weren't shitty by any means. Everyone sat there and listened and applauded like an audience is supposed to do.

What will happen to the group should you end up serving a sentence?

You would have to ask them, but I would hope that since all three of them are excellent musicians, they would go on and create an instrumental sound of their own that didn't depend on lyrics. Until then, we have another album to do. We'll be rehearsing and starting to do that album. Then films have always fascinated me and I'll get into that as quickly as possible and I have another book I want to write.

246

The Interviews: Salli Stevenson

Will you ever write one about the trial?
Maybe I'll write the story of that someday. It might make a good journalistic exercise. One thing that came out of the trial was that I had a chance to get out of L.A. for an extended period of time for the first time in five years. Florida's a beautiful place – unpolluted more or less. I even had a chance to go down to Nassau and learned how to scuba-dive.

I read somewhere that you and the rest of the group owned an island down there.
No, I wish I did because the Caribbean is one of the most beautiful places I've ever visited. The water is perfectly clear and the sand is pure white. The sand out here is brownish in hue and you can see multi-coloured grains, but the sand down there is pure white. It looks like white shells, sea shells, that were ground up very finely. I wish I did own an island down there. They still have land for sale.

KURT: *They have hurricanes too, don't they?*
Yes, it keeps you close to nature. There's a guaranteed calamity every year.

Calamities . . . what about the police?
Police are different in every town and country. Some of the greatest police, unless you get on the wrong side of them, are the English bobbies. They seem to me very civil, gentlemanly kind of cats. The cops in L.A. are different from cops in most towns. They are idealists and they are almost fanatical in believing in the rightness of their cause. They have a whole philosophy behind their tyranny. In most places the police are doing a job, but in L.A. I've noticed a real sense of righteousness about what they are doing which is scary. On the road they're not bad. I was busted once in New Haven, Connecticut. When you are travelling with a band they usually give you hassles, but we're a pretty sedate group, no dopers or sex maniacs or anything like that. So, we have not really run up against too much harrassment. Usually when I go to a strange town, I just stay in the hotel and look out the window anyway.

There have been a lot of different things happening in America. What do you think the outcome for the country will be with the climate as it is now?
I think that whatever happens, America is the arena right now. It's the centre of action and it will take strong, fluid people to survive in a climate like ours. I'm sure people will do it but I think for many people, espcially city dwellers, it's presently a state of constant, total paranoia. As I understand it, paranoia is an irrational fear. The problem is . . . what if the paranoia is real. Then, all you can do is cope with it second by second.

LOS ANGELES
FREE PRESS
Bob Chorush
Spring 1971

This was another one of the last interviews Jim gave
before leaving Los Angeles for France. In it, Jim talked
freely with Bob Chorush – who succeeded John
Carpenter at the *Los Angeles Free Press*
– about his court trials; the new Doors' album then
being recorded, *L.A. Woman*; and a long list of other
subjects, including theatre, film, poetry, reptiles,
shamanism, and alcohol.

'There's no story really. No real narrative. Except there's a hitchhiker who . . . We don't see it, but we later assume that he stole a car
and he drives into the city and it just ends there. He checks into a
motel and he goes out to a nightclub or something. It just kind of
ends like that.'

Jim Morrison is talking about the story of his latest movie HWY. *This
amorphous plot summary seems strangely interchangeable with Morrison's new image of cinema verité director. The James Douglas Morrison
that I spoke to several days ago was an older man than I had expected to
meet. He was a man with grey hairs mingling into his beard and hair, talking about his past as a 'rock star' as a convict might review his past of
'criminal' with a parole officer. A sparkle of the Morrison that I had expected did at times come through, although the flashes were carefully obscured
by the past tense.*

'It always amazes me that people think you're two years younger
than you are. I guess that's why you have to keep doing interviews.
People believe old press clippings. A couple of years ago, I filled a
need that some people had for a figure who represented a whole lot
of things, so they created the thing. It's like seeing baby pictures or
something. It's embarrassing and funny at the same time.'

*My preparation for talking to Morrison included reading three of his
books (*The Lords, The New Creatures *and* An American Prayer*), a
Rolling Stone interview with him and press clippings dating back exactly
four years. I was prepared to meet an alcoholic, drug crazed, megalomania-
cal, slur-speeched, exhibitionist, rock star, film-maker in snakeskin pants
and leather shirt, carrying a celebrated lizard under his arm. The first press
statement that Morrison made laid the groundwork for my misconcep-
tions.*

'You could say it's an accident that I was ideally suited for the
work I am doing. It's the feeling of a bow string being pulled back
for 22 years and suddenly being let go . . . I've always been attracted
to ideas that were about revolt against authority. When you make
your peace with authority you become an authority. I like ideas
about the breaking away or overthrowing of established order. I am

interested in anything about revolt, disorder, chaos, especially activity that seems to have no meaning. It seems to me to be the road towards freedom – external freedom is a way to bring about internal freedom.

'We are from the West. The whole thing should be like an invitation to the West. The sunset. The night. The sea. This is the end. Anything that would promote that image would be useful. The world we suggest should be of a new Wild West. A sensuous evil world. Strange and haunting, the path of the sun . . .'

Morrison is not the image that he has been for so many years. He isn't wearing snakeskin or leather. He has a beer with lunch and a drink before and after. He is his own archer's arrow travelling through the time and space of oblivion with a great deal of insight as to where he's been, and an Indian's aim of where he's going. He is more anxious to talk about films than rock music, a lot of which he no longer listens to. He is also anxious to get the details of his life straight; the most recent of which were his trials on charges ranging from obscenity to plane hijacking. Along with getting straight is the realization that with age, trials and tribulations, has come a loss of naivety.

JIM MORRISON: I wasted a lot of time and energy with the Miami trial. About a year and a half. But I guess it was a valuable experience because before the trial I had a very unrealistic schoolboy attitude about the American judicial system. My eyes have been opened up a bit. There were guys down there, black guys, that would go on each day before I went on. It took about five minutes and they would get 20 or 25 years in jail. If I hadn't had unlimited funds to continue fighting my case, I'd be in jail right now for three years. It's just if you have money you generally don't go to jail. The trial in Miami broke up a lot of things. It's on appeal to the Supreme Court right now.

BOB CHORUSH: *Whatever happened to the other busts that you were involved in?*

I got acquitted on everything else. We're trying to get this erased because it's not good to have something like that on your record.

Are you still concerned with that kind of record?

It's just if something really serious happens then you have a record and it looks a lot worse.

It looked for a while like they were out to get you. There was a federal hijacking charge also, wasn't there?

Well it came under a law that was created because of hijacking, but it wasn't really a hijacking. It was just a little over-exuberant kind of playing. It wasn't a threat to safety or anything. Actually we were acquitted because the stewardesses mistook me for someone who I was with. They were going by the seat number. They were saying that the person in such and such a seat was causing all this trouble. Then they all identified me as being in this seat. They were just trying to hang me because I was the only one that had a well-known face. So they were trying to get me for it. I don't know, I guess it was an example of the kind of people you meet on airplanes.

The trouble with all these busts is that people I know, friends of mine, think it's funny and they like to believe it's true and they accept it; people that don't like me like to believe it because I'm the reincarnation of everything they consider evil. I get hung both ways. I went through a trial there in Phoenix. I had to go back several times to get that cleared up.

What do you think the chances are of getting off in Miami? It's just a misdemeanour now isn't it?

Well, it's two misdemeanours. I have to be optimistic, so I figure there's a good chance. We're going to appeal on several grounds. First of all they never really proved anything except profanity, which we admitted all along. We were going to attempt to prove that profanity did not violate contemporary community standards in the City of Miami. To do that we were going to take the jury to see all the movies like *Woodstock* and *Hair*. *Hair* was playing in town at that time and they had nudity on stage every night and they were allowing young people to go in at any age. And even books that were available in Junior High School libraries had four-letter words. The judge refused to allow any investigation along those lines and limited it to criminal actions. They brought out thirteen witnesses. Every witness was either a policeman who was working there that night or someone who worked for the city and happened to be there, or a relative of a policman. In fact, their biggest witness was a sixteen-year-old girl who was the niece of a police officer who got her and her date in free on that night. All their testimony was very contradictory. Every one of them had a different version of what happened.

I heard that girl called someone 'a little bitch'.

I didn't hear her do it but that's what I heard. They had thousands of photographs from many different people that were there, but there was no photograph of an exposure or anything near it.

The other charges I think were just put in there to make it look more serious. Simulated masturbation, oral copulation . . .
With yourself?
Masturbation on myself and oral copulation on the guitar player. There's a picture of that on the inside sleeve of the *13* album.
Is that a lamb's head you're holding there?
No, that's a real lamb. That guy, Lewis Marvin of the Moonfire, happened to be there. He travels around spreading his philosophy of non-violence and vegetarianism. He carries this lamb around to demonstrate his principles that if you eat meat you're killing this little lamb. He gave it to me during the middle of the show. I just held it for a while. It's interesting. There was a lot of noise, a lot of commotion. It was almost deafening but the lamb was breathing normally, almost purring like a kitten. It was completely relaxed. I guess what they say about lambs to the slaughter is true. They don't feel a thing. Anyway, the judge limited the defence's witnesses to the number of witnesses that the prosecution brought on, which is an entirely arbitrary manoeuvre.
Did you get all those witnesses through an ad?
Yeah, and just through the grapevine. But we had over three hundred people that were willing to testify that they didn't see any of those alleged incidents. What it turns out actually happened is that a journalist happened to be there or heard about this concert and wrote a sensational front page story about the concert, about inciting to riot. The citizens became irate and began calling the police station asking why this had been allowed to go on and why I wasn't arrested. I had gotten up and gone on to Jamaica for a holiday that had been planned there. About three or four days after the whole thing, they swore out a warrant for me. So you can see how the whole thing began.
I spoke to Mike Gershman when he was down there with you and he said that you weren't able to perform during the whole course of the trial. Is it true that you were doing performances?
The only thing I did was the Isle of Wight for a day and then I came right back. We could have done performances but we never knew from one day to the next when court was in session.
They were doing alternate days, weren't they?
Yeah. And he changed it every day. So we never knew. I really needed the weekends to rest up. It was an ordeal.
Do you think they were out to get you or out to get the culture?
I think it was really the lifestyle they were going after. I don't think it was me personally. I just kind of stepped into a hornet's

nest. I had no idea that the sentiment down there was so tender. The audience that was there seemed to enjoy it. I think that the people who read about it in the paper in this distorted version created a climate of hysteria. A few weeks later they had an anti-decency, I mean an anti-indecency, rally at the Orange Bowl with a famous fat comedian.

Well known for his decency.

Right. The President congratulated the kid that started this rally. They had them all over the country.

Did you find yourself excluded from the proceedings the way Manson feels.

Yeah. I felt like a spectator but I wouldn't have wanted to defend myself because I would have blown it, I'm sure. It's not as easy as it looks.

Did you ever get to testify at all?

Yes. I didn't have to testify, but we decided that it might be a good thing for the jury to see what I was like because all they could do is look at me for six weeks or as long as it went. So I testified a couple of days. I don't think it meant anything one way or another. They drag it out so long that after a while no one could care. I suppose that's one of the functions of a trial. They muddle it up so much that you don't know what to think anymore. That's society's way of assimilating a horrible event.

After clearing things up to the present, Morrison seems to feel more at ease about talking about the past. Someone has told me that Morrison used to be close with the Company Theater in Los Angeles until the group did Children of the Kingdom. This play is a study of the thoughts and backstage actions of a 'rock star'. The resemblance between the play's protagonist and Morrison seems to be more than just mere coincidence. The protagonist, like Morrison, tried to realise what was going on in the heads of those that came to see him. Morrison's sense of theatrics had put him in front of a Los Angeles capacity audience reportedly asking 'What do you want? You didn't come here to hear music. What do you want? What do you REALLY want?'

I saw half of *Children of the Kingdom*. I couldn't sit through the rest of it. It made me feel uneasy. Not that I don't appreciate a satire, but it just hit too close to home.

I think people go to rock concerts because they enjoy being in crowds. It gives them a feeling of power and security in a strange way. They like to rub up against hundreds of other people that are like them. It reinforces their trip.

As a performer then, I'm just a focus for everyone's attention, because you have to have an excuse to mob together. Otherwise it becomes a riot.

The Doors never really had any riots. I did try and create something a few times just because I'd always heard about riots at concerts and I mean I thought we ought to have a riot. Everyone else did. So I tried to stimulate a few little riots, you know, and after a few times I realised it's such a joke. It doesn't lead anywhere. You know what, soon it got to the point where people didn't think it was a successful concert unless everybody jumped up and ran around a bit. It's a joke because it leads nowhere. I think it would be better to do a concert and just keep all that feeling submerged so that when everyone left they'd take that energy out on the streets and back home with them. Rather than just spend it uselessly in a little crowd explosion.

No, we never had any real riots. I mean a riot's an out of control, violent thing. We never had too much of what I call a real riot. I think also it has something to do with swarming theory. The idea that when the population starts outstripping the food supply, animals or insects swarm together. It's a way of communicating. Working out a solution or signalling awareness to each other. Signalling that there is a danger. In nature a balance is worked out and I think that somehow that's what's happening. In Los Angeles or New York and many of the big cities, you feel crowded. You feel psychologically crowded and physically crowded. People are getting very neurotic and paranoid and I guess things like rock concerts are a form of human swarming to communicate this uneasiness about overpopulation. I haven't really got it all worked out yet but I think there's something in it.

I think that more than writing music and as a singer, that my greatest talent is that I had an instinctive knack of self-image propagation. I was very good at manipulating publicity with a few little phrases like 'erotic politics'. Having grown up on television and mass magazines, I knew instinctively what people would catch on to. So I dropped those little jewels here and there – seemingly very innocently – of course just calling signals.

I think the Doors were very timely. The music and ideas were very timely. They seem naive now, but a couple of years ago people were into some very weird things. There was a high energy level and you could say things like we did and almost half-ass believe them. Whereas now it seems very naive. I think it was a combination of good musicianship and timeliness. And we may have been one of the first groups to come along who were openly self-conscious of being performers and it was reflected in our career as it was happening.

It's not that we were trend conscious or anything like that. We were doing exactly what we would have been doing anyway. It came at the right time and we could get away with expressing sentiments like that. I'm sure we would have done the same thing anyhow. For example, the first album is not really socially conscious, it's just very universal personal statements. Each album got a little more socially aware of the whole landscape, perhaps to the detriment of the music.

As we travelled and played to large groups of people, then some of the words couldn't help reflecting the things I ran into. That was mainly it. It wasn't any conscious programme. Probably the things we record now will get back to the blues. That's what we do best. We may even do a couple of old blues songs. Just your basic blues.

It'll be good blues. It won't be like a guy with a guitar playing the blues. It will be electric blues, I hope. You never know when you start an album, it could be entirely different. But that's what I'm going to push for. That's the music I enjoy best. It's the most fun to sing. I like jazz too. But you don't need a singer really for jazz. Those guys ought to do some instrumentals. I've always pushed for that. They've been reluctant to do it but I wish they would. Those guys put out a lot of music, a lot of sound for just three guys.

I like any reaction I can get with my music. Just anything to get people to think. I mean if you can get a whole room or a whole club full of drunk, stoned people to actually wake up and think, you're doing something. That's not what they came there for. They came to lose themselves.

I don't know if you saw the set up we have at the office or not. We have a board upstairs. We record right there. It's not that we don't like the Elektra studios, but we felt that we do a lot better when we're rehearsing. We leave a tape running. It's a lot cheaper and faster that way too. This will be the first record that we're actually doing without a producer. We're using the same engineer that we've used, Bruce Botnick. I don't know if he'll be called a producer or not. Probably co-producer with the Doors. In the past, the producer . . . it's not that he was a bad influence or anything, but this will be a lot different without that fifth person there. So anyway, we'll be by ourselves for better or worse.

There were a few new songs on the *Live* album. A year ago we finished *Morrison Hotel*. It's been about a year since we've been in a studio.

A few years ago I wanted to do live performances. I was trying to get everyone to do free surprise spots at the Whisky but no one wanted to. Now everyone wants to, and I totally lost interest. Although I know it's a lot of fun, I just don't have the desire to get up and sing right now. I still enjoy music, but I lost a lot of interest in it.

Are you going to go in more for doing your films?
Yeah, I think so, but there's no hurry on that.

You've done about five films, haven't you?
HWY is the only real film I did. I was involved in the other ones but they weren't totally my films. HWY is, to a large degree. I only see films as a team effort except in a few rare cases. I'd like to get HWY shown. I think maybe it might work on educational television. N.E.T. It's about the right length. You see, it's an uncommercial type film. It's too long for a short play with another feature and it's not a feature itself. It's fifty minutes, an awkward length but I think maybe educational TV might be a good spot for it.

I was always fascinated with a story about a hitchhiker who becomes a mass murderer. I set out to make that film but it turned into a different film. A much more subtle fantasy. Someday, I'd still like to make that hitchhiker film. 'Cause I think it's a good one.

You played the hitchhiker in HWY. *Is acting something you want to get into?*
No, it was just easier that way.

A couple of things that you said about The Lords *interested me, like 'the appeal of cinema lies in the fear of death'. Is that something you can explain?*
I think in art, but especially in films, people are trying to confirm their own existences. Somehow things seem more real if they can be photographed and you can create a semblance of life on the screen. But those little aphorisms that make up most of *The Lords* – if I could have said it any other way I would have. They tend to be mulled over. I take a few seriously. I did most of that book when I was at the film school at U.C.L.A. It was really a thesis on film aesthetics. I wasn't able to make films then, so all I was able to do was think about them and write about them and it probably reflects a lot of that. A lot of the passages in it, for example about shamanism, turned out to be very prophetic several years later because I had no idea when I was writing that I'd be doing just that.

At the end of The Lords, *you define the Lords as the people that are controlling art. Did I understand that right?*
Strangely enough, that's what I meant. Not controlling art neces-

sarily. What that book is a lot about is the feeling of powerlessness and helplessness that people have in the face of reality. They have no real control over events or their own lives. Something is controlling them. The closest they ever get is the television set. In creating this idea of the Lords, it also came to reverse itself. Now to me the Lords mean something entirely different. I couldn't really explain. It's like the opposite. Somehow the Lords are a romantic race of people who have found a way to control their environment and their own lives. They're somehow different from other people.

Is there a particular person you could think of . . .?

No, it's not about any particular person.

I wanted to talk a bit about your poetry also.

Sure, go right ahead.

The New Creatures. *There's a lot of creatures in everything you do. Lizards and snakes and snakeskins. That's part of your reputation. 'The Lizard King'. How did all that come about?*

I had a book on lizards and snakes and reptiles and the first sentence of it struck me acutely – 'reptiles are the interesting descendants of magnificent ancestors'. Another thing about them is that they are a complete anachronism. If every reptile in the world were to disappear tomorrow, it wouldn't really change the balance of nature one bit. They are a completely arbitrary species. I think that maybe they might, if any creature could, survive another world war or some kind of total poisoning of the planet. I think that somehow reptiles could find a way to avoid it.

Does that fit into your own self-concept?

Also, we must not forget that the lizard and the snake are identified with the unconscious and with the forces of evil. That piece 'Celebration of the Lizard' was kind of an invitation to the dark forces. It's all done tongue-in-cheek. I don't think people realise that. It's not to be taken seriously. It's like if you play the villain in a Western it doesn't mean that that's you. That's just an aspect that you keep for show. I don't really take that seriously. That's supposed to be *ironic*.

On a much more basic level, I just always loved reptiles. I grew up in the South-West and I used to catch horned toads and lizards. Of course I still can't get too close to snakes. I mean it's hard for me to pick up a snake and play with it. There's something deep in the human memory that responds strongly to snakes. Even if you've never seen one. I think that a snake just embodies everything that we fear. Basically their skins are just beautiful. I guess that's why they're so fashionable. I think they always have been.

There's probably also a little victory in taking the snake and wearing it.
Yeah, sure. What do they call it – a totem. No, not a totem, a talis-
man. When I wrote *The New Creatures*, I was very naive. It wasn't
something that was born out of any great awareness of the universe.
It's a very naive little book, but somehow a lot of it holds up.
*Do you think you'll be able to do as well on film as you did with the
Doors?*
I don't see why not. I get an instinctive feeling for the film media.
I think I'll do pretty well at it.
*I've noticed that when someone puts down a good film the best reaction
you can get if it's of the same intensity as a Doors concert is that people
walk out on it.*
Well, see, I like that kind of thing. I've never thought that an audi-
ence should be as passive as they've become. I think that an audi-
ence should be an active participant in creating what's happening.
You can even do that with a film. For example, it's up to you to close
your eyes anytime you want or get up and walk out for five minutes. That makes it an entirely different movie than what a person
would see if he sat dutifully through it from beginning to end,
right?
Did you try to do a live performance as part of Feast of Friends *in San
Francisco?*
Did we show that up there? I think we may have at one time. We
showed it at the Aquarius after the concert was over, but that
doesn't mean anything. That was just because we'd made this film
and we felt it was really good and no one would distribute it. So we
just show it when we can. I'm glad we made it. It will be a good document of that era.
*Do you feel that people are more willing to accept your films or more
willing to reject them knowing your notoriety or your background as a
singer?*
I think that I may get a chance to do a film because of that notoriety. I'll probably get *one* chance. If it doesn't really make it, it will
probably be very hard to get another chance. But I think that almost
anyone can get one chance nowadays to make some kind of film.
Do you find that your reputation as 'rock singer' gets in the way?
They always want a soundtrack or they even have the audacity to
want you to play a singer for the movie. I'm not really interested in
acting. It doesn't bother me that much.
What's your reputation as a drinker?
[Long pause] I went through a period where I drank a lot. I had a
lot of pressures hanging over me that I couldn't cope with. I think

also that drinking is a way to cope with living in a crowded environment, and also a product of boredom. I know people drink because they're bored. I enjoy drinking. It loosens people up and stimulates conversation sometimes. It's like gambling somehow, you go out for a night of drinking and you don't know where you're going to end up the next day. It could work out good or it could be disastrous. It's like the throw of the dice.

There seem to be a lot of people shooting smack and speed and all that now. Everybody smokes grass – I guess you don't consider that a drug anymore. Three years ago there was a wave of hallucinogenics. I don't think anyone really has the strength to sustain those kicks forever. Then you go into narcotics, of which alcohol is one. Instead of trying to think more you try and kill thought with alcohol and heroin and downers. These are pain killers. I think that's what people have gotten into. Alcohol for me, because it's traditional. Also, I hate scoring. I hate the kind of sleazy sexual connotations of scoring from people so I never do that. That's why I like alcohol, you can go down to any corner store or bar and it's right across the table.

I think what happens now is that people smoke so much and so constantly that it's not a trip anymore. I think they build up a cellular tolerance for it. It just becomes part of their body chemistry. They're not really stoned.

Morrison talks on. Always conscious about his image. Relaxed. He is fascinated by a mini-skirted girl who gets out of a car across the street, and by Zap Comix. *He wants to write about his trial and wonders where he should submit his story. He drops hints about a friend of his who could be the world's greatest female vocalist. He seems nervous about getting back to the studio. He's already two hours late. But . . .*

There is no story really. No real narrative . . . he drives into the city . . . he goes out . . . or something . . . it just kind of ends like that . . . and . . . when the music's over, turn off the lights . . .

Jim Morrison's film career is about to begin.

ROLLING STONE

Ben Fong-Torres

Spring 1971

The Doors were recording their final album *L.A. Woman*, as a quartet, when one of *Rolling Stone*'s pre-eminent interviewers, Ben Fong-Torres, talked to them in Los Angeles. With the Miami trial finally behind him, Jim was now free to talk about it. The article was published in March 1971, shortly before Jim went to Paris.

The Lizard King

Los Angeles – Jim Morrison and the Doors are back home in Hollywood and at work on an album – this time without producer Paul Rothchild, and this time featuring 'blues', Morrison says, 'original blues, if there's such a thing'.

Morrison, the ex-sex symbol of West Coast rock; the poet who called himself 'Lizard King' is a convicted man, following a two month trial in Florida for his alleged organ recital at a March, 1969 concert in Miami. He was found guilty of misdemeanours – indecent exposure and open profanity – and his case is on appeal – probably for an indefinite time. He's out on bail.

Jim Morrison, all of the above, is still a Door. He continues the transition from rock'n'roll to poetry and films. And he has aged. His face is still jungular, but now more lion-like than Tarzanic, outlined as it is by comfortably long dark hair and full, dark beard. And he's got the beginning of a beer belly. Quiet about his Miami case in the Rolling Stone *interview he did in July 1969 and silent, still, during the trial, Morrison seemed eager to talk a bit when we ran into each other in Hollywood – to put the old days in proper perspective, to discuss the Doors, and to assess the whole Miami thing, in his own words.*

BEN FONG-TORRES: *Do you still consider yourself the 'Lizard King'?*

JIM MORRISON: That was two years ago, and even then it was kind of ironic. I meant it ironically . . . half tongue-in-cheek. It was an easy thing to pick up on. I just thought everyone knew it was ironic, but apparently they thought I was mad.

Do you think you'd be classified among the people who signify what some people insist is the 'death of rock'?

Well, I was saying rock is dead years ago. What rock means to me is – for example, in one period 20 or 30 years ago, jazz was the kind of music people went to, and large crowds danced to and moved around to. And then rock'n'roll replaced that, and then another generation came along and they called it rock. The new generation of kids will come along in a few years, swarm together, and have a new name for it. It'll be the kind of music that people like to go out and get it on to.

But back 20, 30 years ago the music didn't become a symbol of a whole new culture or subculture.

But, you know, each generation wants new symbols, new people, new names – they want to divorce themselves from the preceding generation; they won't call it rock . . . Don't you see a cyclical thing every five or ten years, when everyone comes together and swarms and breaks apart . . . When you think of rock, it's not mind music. I mean, if you couldn't understand the words, there'd still be everything there to react to.

How about Miami? Will that whole thing affect whether you'll play any more concerts?

I think that was the culmination, in a way, of our mass performing career. Subconsciously, I think I was trying to get across in that concert – I was trying to reduce it to absurdity, and it worked too well.

When did it stop getting to be fun?

I think there's a certain moment when you're right in time with your audience and then you both grow out of it and you both have to realise it; it's not that you've outgrown your audience; it has to go on to something else.

You see blues fitting in with this?

No, it's just getting back to more of what we enjoy. What we actually personally enjoy. Not that we've ever not played music that we didn't like. When we were playing clubs, I'd say over half of what we did was blues, and we used our own material on records, but I think the most exciting things we did were basic blues. I like them mainly 'cause they're fun to sing.

We're using Elvis' bass player – his name is Jerry, damn it, I forget his last name [Scheff] – and for the first time we recorded it in our office where we rehearse, and the board's upstairs; we're using the engineer that we used on the other records – Bruce Botnick – but we're not using Paul Rothchild on this one. It was kind of mutual; just figured it was time . . . to take different roads.

What was your main interest in the Miami case, aside from your personal liberty?

You know, I was hoping – or I thought there might be a possibility of it becoming a major, ground-breaking kind of case, but it didn't turn out that way. It might have been one of the reasons why they dragged it out so long in order not to let enough momentum or sentiment build up in a short time, or a lot of attention focus on it. So it actually received very little national attention. But in a way I was kind of relieved, because as the case wore on, there were no great ideals at stake.

I thought it might become just a basic American issue involving

freedom of speech and the right of anyone with a personal view-
point to state their ideas in public and receive a hearing without legal pressure being put on them. In fact my lawyer made a
speech part way through the trial in which he traced the origin of
freedom of speech which goes side by side with the origin of drama,
actually. The right of the dramatist or artist to state his views. It was
a brilliant summary of that historical process, but it didn't have
any effect on the outcome at all. The first amendment provides supposedly for the freedom of expression. There's a clause which states
that any dramatic or public artistic performance comes under this
amendment.

Basically the prosecution refused to listen to any testimony which
would come under that clause. They were prosecuting totally on a
criminal case. My defence counsel was prepared to put the whole
case on the fact that even if this alleged event did occur, it did not
violate contemporary community standards, and they were going
to take the jury to see *Woodstock*, a lot of other films – and during the
trial the production company of *Hair* opened up in Miami, and they
had obscenity and full nudity on stage in it, and there were no
restrictions on it as to the age of the audience – they let anybody in
– but the judge anticipated that, and he threw out the proceedings.

But is that a really relevant parallel? In Hair, *say, that profanity and
that alleged obscenity is planned as part of the act. Would you then have to
testify that whatever acts you took were part of your act? Yours were spontaneous.*

But it is a theatrical performance, nonetheless. It's not a political
rally. We go on to a series of songs that everyone's familiar with.
The people who come to the shows have the albums and I think
they know basically what they're coming to see.

I suppose they could've had a point there, but they never even
got into that.

What did they find you guilty of?

There were four charges – one was a felony which carried a three
year rap – for lascivious behaviour including exposure. And three
misdemeanours – one was on profanity; one was on – let's see – oh,
public drunkenness, and the other was one which included the
exposure charge; it was a separate one. So constitutionally, right
there they were wrong. You're not supposed to be able to try a person on the same count twice. You could argue that anyway. That's
probably one of the motions that we'll include in the appeal.

*Why wasn't that argued in the very beginning? Couldn't you have
called for a dismissal of the trial?*

Yeah, we called for a dismissal a score of times, but they were all denied.

Another cause for argument was that there was no possible way I could have received a fair trial because of the climate of public opinion that had been stirred up for a year and a half – probably a newspaper story or a radio or TV story in Miami. We have a sheaf of clippings that takes up two files from all over the country. But one thing I was interested to observe: every day we would rush home to watch ourselves on TV; they couldn't film in the court room, but going and leaving they'd film it, and we'd hear the reporters' views of what had happened. The first few days it was kinda the old-line policy, what people had been thinking for a year and a half, but as the trial wore on, the reporters themselves, from just talking to me and the people involved in the case – the tone of the news articles – and even the papers – became a little more objective as each day went on.

What's in the immediate future for the Doors? Any concerts?

No, we're kind of off playing concerts; somehow no one enjoys the big places anymore, and to go into clubs more than just a night every now and then is kind of meaningless. I think we'll do a couple of albums and then everyone will probably get into their own thing; each guy in the band has certain projects that they want to do more independently. I heard that Robbie would like one on his own, predominantly a guitar thing, and John has always been – basically he likes jazz, and I would suspect he might produce and play in a jazz album. Robbie and John a couple of years ago produced an album of some friends of theirs called *A Comfortable Chair*; they've both got an ear for producing.

How about yourself? Do you have a film project?

Ahhh . . . I guess that's what I've always wanted to do, even more than being in a band, was working in films. I'd like to write and direct a film of my own – there's one that's all in my head, but I have a film which I made, which hasn't been seen very much, it's called *HWY*.

Wasn't it shown up in Canada at a 'Jim Morrison Film Festival'? How did it go over?

The reports I got were that *HWY* was very enthusiastically received.

That wasn't the case in San Francisco at the film festival there . . .

Feast of Friends was shown there a year or so ago with a lot of boos. I think they were reacting to personalities rather than the film. *HWY* was entered in the San Francisco Film Festival, but it was rejected, for whatever reason. It's a 50 minute film, 35 millimeter, and in colour. I act in it and made it with some friends of mine. It's more poetic, more of an exercise for me, kind of a warm up. There's no story in it. Just a hitchhiker who steals a car . . . we assume that, anyway . . . and he drives into town and checks into a motel or something and it just kind of ends like that.

LAST WORDS

IN THE SPRING of 1971, just months before he died, Jim hand-scrawled a letter to Dave Marsh, who was then the editor of *Creem* magazine. Jim used a lined notepad and his script was large, so that he wrote on every other line. Sometimes he would cross out words and phrases. His vocabulary was simple, the sentences taut and flat like Ernest Hemingway's. Marsh had asked about the new album then being recorded. Jim answered the question and then, typically, threw in some philosophy:

He started the letter off with a simple technical description of the making of the album – in their 'rehearsal studio w/an 8-track in the office upstairs', producing it themselves with Bruce Botnick as engineer and co-producer. There's a feeling of satisfaction, excitement even, in the straightforward statement that 'This is a blues album'.

'The songs have a lot to do w/ America & what it's like to live these years in L.A.,' he wrote, adding that he saw the city as a 'genetic blue-print' for the United States. He admitted in the letter that he had had the 'fortunate' chance to work out a personal myth there, a 'late adolescent phantasy [sic] on reality terms at large'. After mentioning *HWY* and other things that he was working on, including 'a long essay on the Trial in Florida', he signed off:

> 'I am not mad.
> I am interested
> in freedom.
> Good luck.
> J Morrison'

ACKNOWLEDGEMENTS

I would like to thank John Tobler for originally commissioning this book some years ago. Thanks to my publishers Sandra Wake and Terry Porter at Plexus Publishing for being instrumental in making it finally happen and to Nicky Adamson for her role as editor, midwife and mother. Without their unflagging effort and meticulous attention to detail the many loose ends would have remained untied forever.

I would also like to thank the writers, and editors, who contributed their Morrison interviews: Art Kunkin, Bob Chorush, the late John Carpenter, Salli Stevenson, Jerry Rothberg, John Tobler, Richard Goldstein, Ben Fong-Torres and Jann Wenner. Thanks also to the original publications: *Rolling Stone* magazine and Straight Arrow Publishers Inc, *Circus* magazine and Circus Enterprizes Corp, *Zigzag* magazine and the *Los Angeles Free Press*.

Acknowledgement for help with research and in assembling the interviews and visual material to: Jeannie Cromie, Diane Gardiner, Robert Klein, Art Kunkin, Rainer Moddemann, Hervé Muller, Patricia Keneally Morrison, Danny Sugerman, Dave Marsh, Stephen Adamson, Sandra Cowell, Harvey Weinig and Jann Wenner. And to Corinne Brinkman for translating the Paris documents concerning Morrison's death.

Finally grateful thanks to the following photographers: Joel Brodsky and Elektra Records for the cover photograph; Robert Klein pages 14, 42, 47, 50/51, 61, 62, 68, 83; Ed Caraeff pages 6, 13, 17, 52, 55, 58, 67, 79, 90, 126, 262; David Sygall pages 23, 27, 72, 210; Baron Wolman pages 24, 94, 107, 123; Mike Barich pages 2, 88/89, 107, 118, 261, 268; Gloria Stavers/Starfile/Pictorial Press pages 20, 31, 76; Raeanne Rubenstein/People in Pictures pages 28, 142; Joseph Sia pages 102, 109, 113, 153; Jeff Simon pages 131, 135; WEA/Elektra Records/Paul Ferrara page 188; WEA/Elektra Records/Edmund Teske page 216; WEA/Elektra Records/Jeff Simon page 248; Andrew Kent page 158; Claude Gassian pages 177, 185; Barry Plummer pages 201, 230; Don Paulsen page 8/9; UPI Bettmann Newsphotos page 101; the US Navy Public Information Office pages 35, 41; Araldo di Crollalanza pages 114, 202; Edmund Teske page 147; Hervé Muller pages 163, 166, 171; Jane Hopkins page 238; George Washington High School, Virginia page 38; Chris Walter page 65; Steen Kaersgaard page 98/99; Peter Saunders page 105; the Department of State Foreign Service of the United States of America page 175; Sounds page 237.

Jerry Hopkins, 1992

272